Crisis and the Renewal of Creation

Crisis and the Renewal of Creation

WORLD AND CHURCH IN THE AGE OF ECOLOGY

*Edited by Jeffrey Golliher
and William Bryant Logan*

CONTINUUM • NEW YORK

1996
The Continuum Publishing Company
370 Lexington Avenue
New York, NY 10017

Printed in the United States of America

Library of Congress Cataloging in Publication Data

Crisis and the renewal of creation : world and church in the age of
  ecology / edited by Jeffrey Golliher and William Bryant Logan.
      p.   cm.
  Ecological sermons delivered at the Cathedral of St. John the
Divine in New York, N.Y.
    ISBN 0-8264-0798-6 (hardcover : alk. paper)
    1. Human ecology—Religious aspects—Christianity—Sermons.
  2. Environmental ethics—Sermons. 3. Episcopal Church—Sermons.
  4. Sermons, American.   I. Golliher, Jeffrey.   II. Logan, William
  Bryant.   III. Cathedral of St. John the Divine (New York, N.Y.)
  BT695.5.C75   1995
  261.8'362—dc20   95-23770
                                                                 CIP

ACKNOWLEDGMENTS
The publication of this volume has been made possible by generous
grants from the Bishop Robert L. Paddock Trust, the René Dubos
Foundation, the Arthur and Barbara Crocker Charitable Trust, the
Educational Foundation of America, and Mr. Drake Darrin. Many grate-
ful thanks are offered for their support.

Contents

IV / STEWARDSHIP AND RENEWAL

Introduction

DEAN JAMES PARKS MORTON

Today we live in the face of the most profound environmental crises that the planet has ever confronted. We have at last realized that ecology is not a fifth wheel in our reflections about the human role on Earth.

The fact is, though, that this consciousness is so new, it has only begun to sink in. It wasn't until the summer of 1988—that very hot summer when medical wastes washed up on our beaches and when that barge full of garbage wandered the globe searching for a place to dump its load—that matters of ecology went from being page 37 news to front-page headlines. Only then did ecology emerge from the think-tanks and appear at the breakfast table all over America.

That was the summer when *Newsweek* ran a cover that showed the typical American family under a bell jar representing the Greenhouse Effect (as if it were a new discovery when in fact our brighter scientists had been warning about it for decades). And at the end of the year, *Time* magazine replaced its usual Man of the Year award with a Planet of the Year award, splashing the photograph of a Christo-wrapped Earth seen from the Moon across its most-read cover of the year.

Before that time only those perceived as fanatics—such as members of Friends of the Earth, the Sierra Club, or the NRDC—regarded the environment as a crucial issue. And the churches of America, by and large, were just as backward as the general public. So the media and the Church—the two institutions most clearly charged with bearing the "Good News"—didn't know it or convey it until those important events of 1988.

At the Cathedral of St. John the Divine in New York City, I have been stressing the importance of ecological thinking for two decades. We have done everything in our power to wake up churches and individuals since 1974. The sermons and talks presented in this book represent some of the fruit of these twenty years of work.

It is only recently that churches themselves have begun to concur on the importance of the issue. We forced them to pay attention by finally persuading the higher-ups in American religious institutions to meet and consult with top scientists to assess and acknowledge both the depth of the ecological crisis and the need for the matter to be at the center of spiritual life.

The Joint Appeal in Religion and Science—our pioneer group that has blossomed now into the National Religious Partnership for the Environment—takes the issue of ecological stewardship into 53,000 parishes and synagogues around the country.

But what is this dawning ecological consciousness in itself? One of its components is thinking that is political and issue-driven, related to the need to address and regulate toxins, soil loss, the pollution of our aquifers, and many such specific issues. A second, equally crucial component involves the crucial lifestyle changes that must be made: recycling must become as consistent a ritual for us as saying our prayers.

The third—and deepest—component of the new consciousness is the acknowledgment of the interconnectedness of everything. Here, we recognize the fragility of living systems, their mutual strength, and their mutual vulnerability. Indeed, the growing environmental consciousness is very close to spirituality itself, for religion is essentially the yearning in the human heart and the human brain for inclusiveness, wholeness, togetherness.

In the twenty-two sermons that follow, you will hear some of the prophet ic voices that have made this connection between religion and ecology, and have begun the reflection that can bring our hearts abreast of the times.

✦ I ✦
THE TROUBLE
WE'VE SEEN

The Lichen Sermon

RENÉ DUBOS and
DEAN JAMES PARKS MORTON

DEAN MORTON: With Professor Dubos we want to look at poverty and the lesson of today's Gospel in relation to science, particularly in relation to Professor Dubos' disciplines of biology and ecology. In a sense, today's Gospel is the perfect take-off place for an ecologist, for the Gospel is the multiplication of the loaves and the fishes.

The multiplication of the loaves and the fishes is a gift to be shared. But look at the reverse of any gift! There is the temptation to say that it is not a gift. And the reverse of the gift, indeed, comes in the last sentence of the Gospel. The people said, "This is the prophet who is to come into the world." And our Lord, perceiving that they were coming to take him by force and make him a king, left them immediately.

This is precisely the lesson Dostoyevsky taught in the story of the Grand Inquisitor. Turn the bread giver into a king—a spectacular machine for production. Just let the bread keep coming, and we will not have to share. Sharing is a spiritual discipline, therefore, that can exist only in the context of scarcity or poverty.

So we ask you, Mr. Dubos. For an understanding of this Gospel of sharing as a spiritual discipline, we turn to science. Do you find a relation in your disciplines between sharing and poverty? Do you have any evidence that poverty is ever anything more than deprivation? In nature, is poverty ever creative or positive?

DR. DUBOS: First, let me acknowledge that I have great difficulty in understanding deep in my heart the theological meaning that you give to the word, *poverty*. I had always assumed, and I supppose many of you believe, that poverty is deprivation, a deprivation of worldy goods, a deprivation of satisfying human contacts. Even though I began during the past two weeks—following my conversations with you, Dean Morton—sensing that there was something more than that concept of poverty, it is only very recently— the day before yesterday, in fact—that I came to realize that within my own scientific discipline, that of biology, there are many indications that scarcity is not only creative but is essential to the act of creation.

So what I am going to do now, if you allow me, is to behave according to that long conditioning of academic life and begin by presenting the topic in an abstract way, fortunately, however, through the form of a parable! I will then try to translate these abstract considerations into the terms of the problems of our society today.

Let me begin with the parable. It is a biological parable. I shall invite you to walk with me almost anywhere in the world. Wherever there are trees, where there are rocks, or the stone walls of old buildings. If you look at those rocks, at those trunks, at those old stone walls, at those old buildings, you will see that their surface is commonly covered with a kind of growth, exhibiting all sorts of colors, all sorts of different structures, often incredibly beautiful. You all have seen them, and possibly you have used the word *moss*. What I am speaking about are not mosses. It is what biologists and many of you recognize as *lichens*.

Now, you will say, "Well, lichens are just small plants." And that is what scientists used to believe. But one now knows that lichens are in reality an association of two very lowly kinds of microbes: a mold and a microscopic algae. And the remarkable thing, which will be the theme of my parable, is that when these two lowly microbes become associated, in a single organism so to speak, they develop multiplicities of beautiful and complex forms, beautiful subtle colors. They create all sorts of new chemicals (many of them being used for the perfume industry), and they acquire all sorts of new properties that one could not have anticipated from just considering the mold or the microscopic algae all by itself.

We see then that each of these lowly microbes has the potential power to produce all sorts of wonderful forms, all sorts of wonderful qualities. But this potential becomes expressed only when the two become intimately associated. So the first lesson I derive from my parable is that associating and working together is essential throughout life for the creation of new values.

Now there is a second part of the lesson, one perhaps more directly and obviously relevant to the problem of poverty, namely this: if there is too much food, then the microbes stop their association: they start growing on their own. They do not find the need to associate, to help each other. Separately they continue growing as a mold or as a microscopic algae, but there is nothing interesting about them. Abundance, excessive abundance, makes them return to a dull, uninspiring kind of life. Thus, in a peculiar way, the lichens in their richness are an expression of the poverty of the environment in which they develop.

What I have described here for lichens has been recognized for nearly one hundred years. The word for this kind of association, invented at the time, is *symbiosis*. This Greek word means "living together." In reality it is more than just living together, it is working together, becoming integrated into one single organism.

Let us skip for a moment the word *symbiosis*. Let us look about at nature, and we shall see wherever we look, at any level of development in living things, that there are countless such forms of association and cooperation. They have been expressed by all sorts of words. One phrase very popular half a century ago was invented by the Russian sociologist Kropotkin. He spoke of the "mutual aid" between different living things existing under difficult conditions. If you now transfer this concept to human life, you will see that, without any difficulty, you arrive at the word *communion*. In fact the word *communion* is the exact equivalent in Latin of the Greek word *symbiosis*. I derive from my parable the conclusion that communion is more than just being associated. It is not only sharing, it is sharing in such a way that one engages in creative interplay. You can apply the word *communion* to all sorts of situations. You can think of communion with nature, communion with other human beings, and of course, you can think of communion with the cosmos as a whole and thereby arrive at the large theological sense—the divine sense—of the word *communion*.

DEAN MORTON: You would say then that communion is possible only if there is an *openness*, which I use as another word for *poverty*. The human tendency, more often than not, is to build a wall so that my goods will not be stolen, as opposed to being open and vulnerable. *Vulnerability* is another word for this openness, for poverty.

The rhetoric of our society says that the good life is posited upon more and more and more. This is, we are coming to recognize, a very energy-expensive society. Professor Dubos, must we be so extravagent with energy? Could you apply poverty, as you have shown it at work in nature, to our energy economy?

DR. DUBOS: As you all know, in public discussions about energy or about resources, the only consideration is how much of it we can get, how much it will cost, what will the bad effects be of any kind of shortage. Now, I am not unaware of the problems caused by shortage of resources and of energy. What is important, however is not how much we have, it is how we use it. Paradoxical as it may sound, we often do damage to the world and to our own lives by excessive use of resources and energy. In many cases, creativity demands that we limit our consumption of both.

Let me take three very concrete examples. I have selected them not for theoretical reasons but because they are problems from our life today. The three examples that I have selected deal with agriculture, with architecture, and with our physical and mental health.

Speaking about agriculture, I must become a bit pedantic, once more acting in my profession as an academician. I shall ask you to think of those many parts of the world where more than twenty thousand years ago people created the land out of the wilderness and have used it extensively ever since, not only maintaining its quality and beauty, but even enhancing it by their management. During the past fifty years or so we have decided that we can change all that, that we can greatly increase the productivity of agriculture by pumping energy into the system, whether in the form of high-power equipment like tractors and whatnot or in the form of synthetic fertilizers and pesticides. I know how beneficial this has been; I know how dependent we are on the intelligent use of these forms of energy for the production of food for the world as a whole. I also know, however, that if we are careless in our use of energy and resources in agriculture, we destroy the very system upon which we depend.

It is well known, scientifically (and the ancient farmers knew it empirically), that the soil, natural soil, has fundamental biological mechanisms which enable it to produce humus and accumulate numerous fertilizers. There exist in the soil certain kinds of microbes that capture the nitrogen from the air and feed it into plants. We are learning that as soon as we pump too much energy into agricultural systems, we tend to inhibit the expression of those fundamental mechanisms. Humus gets destroyed, and the bacteria that fix the nitrogen from the air can no longer function. So here we see a situation where too much energy prevents the expression of the recuperative and curative natural mechanisms of the soil.

Now, the case of architecture. Until about fifty years ago, all over the world, builders and architects used to adapt their structures to local constraints: the shape of the roof, the thickness of the walls, the type of windows, the orientation of the building. All this was determined by the snow, the rainfall, the winds, the temperature, and so on. From their awareness of the fundamental constraints imposed by the environment, the architects of old—and, for that matter, ordinary people—had developed local architecture everywhere that, with respect to Dean Morton's question, had an immense variety and charm, that was very comfortable, that was inexpensive in its use of energy. (Those of you who would be entertained by reading on this topic should look at *Architecture without Architects,* a book that shows how people over the years had the sense to build to suit natural conditions.) Well, during the past fifty years, as I said, we have been pumping energy into our buildings so as to avoid respecting those constraints. We have become so careless in our use of energy that we overheat our buildings during the winter and overcool them during the summer. All this results in the anonymous kind of architecture that disgraces all of our cities all over the world.

I have no doubt that if we become more economical, more reasonable, in the use of energy we can once more give to architecture the kind of quality that depends upon its being suited to local conditions.

DEAN MORTON: You could use just another word again: *communion.* The New York glass skyscraper, with windows that cannot open, precisely refuses communion with the environment. It refuses the symbiotic back-and-forth vulnerability. It is a sort of shaking the fist at environmental architecture. To hell with the environment in which it sits!

DR. DUBOS: The last example I want to give is about our physical and mental health. Without being professional biologists, you all know that we are born with a wide range of potentialities, physical and mental. You also know that those potentialities become expressed only to the extent that we give them a chance to function.

Just think of muscle. Each one of us is born with the potential for vigorous muscles, but those muscles become vigorous only to the extent that we exercise them. This is just as true for all the other functions of our body. Children are born with the ability to learn, to experience, and to love. These potential gifts that we have at birth become reality only to the extent we make the effort to learn to share with other people and to experience the loveliness of nature.

My personal feeling is that during the past one hundred years or so there has been an increasing tendency in all Western societies, increasingly all over the world, to use energy only to avoid effort instead of using energy to experience the world with our bodies and with all the faculties of our minds.

So to be very dogmatic (for lack of time), our physical and mental health depends in a large measure on the extent to which we use our potentialities and begin to express them as early as possible. If we could rearrange our society in such a manner that we do not spend energy to avoid effort but spend our energy to become involved—in things of man and nature—we would improve our physical health and our mental health.

DEAN MORTON: Could you, in conclusion, Professor Dubos, say something about the place of human beings within the larger creative order, within this understanding of communion and of poverty?

DR. DUBOS: This is the kind of question that I formulate for myself and, usually, only answer to myself. To answer such a question I would have to go way beyond the field of knowledge that I have mastered and . . .

DEAN MORTON: . . . become a theologian!

DR. DUBOS: ... and have to engage in interpretations of a very highly personal nature. So let me again speak from a parable, namely, the biblical parable that Adam was created from the Earth. For me, as a biologist, there is a very deep scientific meaning in this parable. It is a symbol of the fact that we were created as a species and that we each create ourselves as individuals by functioning within the natural order of Creation, by experiencing all of Creation during our evolutionary development as a species and during our individual development as people. So, in this scientific kind of explanation I have rediscovered or restated the words of the Greek theologian, Origen, who said that man is the mirror of the cosmos.

From this I derive the conclusion, which I try to apply to my own life, that we are healthy— and the word *healthy* has an etymological relationship to the word *whole*—only to the extent that we participate actively with our own energy, with that energy which is us, in the life of nature and in the life of other human beings.

DEAN MORTON: We could push the etymology just one step further: health, wholeness, holiness! Amen.

March 9, 1975

Social and Environmental Denial

JOHN KENNETH GALBRAITH and
DEAN JAMES PARKS MORTON

DEAN MORTON: The 1992 Rio meeting of the United Nations Conference on Environment and Development called UNCED was really a watershed in the history of the world. What Rio taught the world was that all life was interdependent; that we have to think of the total planet, of wholeness; we have to think of development and poverty at the same time that we think of the environment. We have to think of the southern hemisphere whenever we think of the northern hemisphere. We have to keep rich nations and poor nations together. What affects one effects all.

That's the basic word of Rio. The image of the planet taken from the moon is truly our icon for our world. It drives home the Christian understanding of all together, the Corpus Christi or the body of Christ in which every member needs every other member. The secretary-general of the Rio Conference is a Cathedral colleague, a former trustee of the Cathedral, Maurice Strong, and he said Rio is all about economics: about how we live together, of how we make our planet work.

Now to start with, both Jeremiah and St. Paul in his letter to Timothy, which is the Epistle, are testimonies of men who have been slugging it out and who almost lost—of two men who were genuinely overwhelmed. Look at the words of Jeremiah: "Have you completely rejected Judah? Does your heart, Oh Lord, loathe Zion? Why have you struck us down so there is no healing for us? We look for peace but find no good.

We look for healing but there is terror instead." Or look at Paul to Timothy: "I have been poured out as a libation. The time of my departure is at hand. All have deceived me." These are men speaking of desperation. And yet, both Jeremiah and Paul end by saying: Can any idols of the nations bring rain? Or can the heavens give showers? Is it not you, Oh Lord our God, we set our hope on you. For it is you who do all this for Paul. So I was rescued from the lion's mouth. The Lord will rescue me from every evil attack and save me for the heavenly kingdom. Both men were slugging it out, and both men put their ultimate trust in God.

The second lesson, the Gospel, is the Pharisee and the publican. One is a proud man who genuinely sees himself set apart from the rest of humanity. That's the Pharisee. And he says, "I thank God that I'm not like other people." You see a person here who is a despiser of the unfortunate. A despiser of stereotypes. A despiser of the poor. And on the other hand, you see the tax collector. I suppose in modern English the tax collector is a despised position, someone like a traffic ticket agent, or possibly an IRS agent. The point about this despised man is his humility and his solidarity with all people. He doesn't justify himself as better than others, but instead he beats his breast and says, "God be merciful to me, a sinner." And Jesus said, "This is the man who is justified and not the Pharisee who said he was better than everyone else." We are responsible. As Harvard professor Timothy C. Weiskel puts it:

> It is only through a fundamental reformulation of our religiously held beliefs and a thorough transformation of our public policy that we, the entire human species, will have any realistic chance of long-time survival in the twenty-first century. . . . We are in big trouble; truly terrifying trouble. Trouble from which—on our own—it is not likely that we will ever fully recover. It seems as if humankind is at war with the natural world. . . . Listen. The good news and the bad news is that we are winning. The tragedy is that by winning, we lose. Without some strong and governing principle of limit, we are likely to lose in a big way.

And so, dear friends, facing economy, facing the environment, facing poverty, we are facing the overwhelming challenges that overwhelmed both Jeremiah and Paul. Keep the image of the Pharisee and the publican in your mind and say, what does the Gospel bring to my sensitivity as a citizen?

PROFESSOR GALBRAITH: It is thirty-five years since I first found myself concerned with environmental issues and began writing about them. I was then, as I remain, considerably concerned with visual pollution: The diversely ugly commercialism that assails our eyes along our highways and, more generally, in our cities. And, in what has been a too-often quoted passage, I wrote at the time and I quote:

> The family that takes this mauve and cerise air-conditioned power-steered and power-braked automobile out for a tour, passes through cities that are badly paved, made hideous by litter, blighted buildings, billboards, and posts and wires that should have been long-since put underground.
>
> They pass on into a countryside which has been rendered largely invisible by commercial art. They picnic on exquisitely packaged food from a portable icebox by a polluted stream and go on to spend the night at a park which is a menace to public health and morals. Just before dozing off on air mattresses beneath a nylon tent, amid the stench of decaying refuse, they may reflect vaguely on the curious unevenness of their blessings. Is this indeed the American genius?

In ensuing years, I became involved in the war against billboard affliction, a battle, which early on, we won in the state of Vermont. And elsewhere now, roadsides are somewhat better protected. I do not take much encouragement from this, for on the larger issues of the environment, we are still losing ground. The problem is still ahead of the protective and remedial action that is needed.

There is, I believe, a deeper reason why we are losing. It involves a dysfunction in our economic and social system: one that we seek to deny, or in any case, that we find convenient to overlook. There is a difference in economic incidence and cost and in time, between those who pay for social action and those who now or later, stand in need of that action. Once the rich and generally affluent were few; a democracy could tax them with pleasant political sanction. Now the rich and the affluent are numerous and politically dominant. Taxes, in consequence, have become a grave oppression. We see this dysfunction everyday in our central cities.

It is in our inner cities that people most urgently need social support for education, for housing, for drug counseling, for law enforcement, for the basic monetary requisites of human survival. It is the more affluent of our community who bear the cost and inevitably so.

But out of this comes a solemn, self-serving doctrine: the poor are morally damaged by the help so accorded. The poor are also a heavy burden on government and society. So it is said. Even more expensive government functions that serve the more fortunate of our community are, however, not a burden. Defense expenditures, social security, the bailing out of failed financial institutions and interest on the public debt (those that are more important for the fortunate of our people), these functions are necessarily not a burden and are an approved action by the state. The poor, it is held, are morally damaged by public services and support while what government does for the affluent is necessary, sound, and justified.

The case of the environment is only slightly different. Here, too, the cost of environmental protection is now; the protection and reward is for those who come later. We pay now for future benefit. And those who so benefit are a different generation from those who now pay. And so, we have the problem: the cost is for us, the benefit is for others, including many yet unborn.

As taxation for the poor is a burden, so is the cost of environmental regulation and expenditure for generations yet to come. As deeply immoral and visibly fraudulent reasons are found for opposing help to the poor, so also are such reasons found for opposing the cost of protecting the environment. It cannot be said that future generations should be allowed to suffer in their own way. No one can contend that life on the planet should be impaired, perhaps sacrificed, to present public economy and contentment. To say that would be obviously too obvious, too indecent.

So, opposition to environmental protection has its contrived litany, its escapist doctrine: more research is always needed to establish the true extent of the environmental threat. Economic competitiveness may be impared. Jobs may be lost by environmental action. Government must not intrude on the sacred precincts of the free enterprise system.

It would be a relief, on occasion, to hear the real case, which is, that we live in the present and that we simply say that the future may never come. Or let us hear someone say, "We simply do not want to pay the price." In my now adequately mature years, I do not have great hope of major change. I have a more conscientious concern for the poor and for the environment, and a willingness to pay the price. I believe the resisting attitudes to be very strong, and those who have those resisting attitudes also have political voice. But at least one can identify the sordid situation: it is nothing but self-regard and selfishness under a deeply implausible disguise. Removing that cloak, seeing the underlying reality, has its own rude reward.

In the Name of the Wounded Sky

ROBERT KINLOCH MASSIE, JR.

[*The following text is a slightly revised version of the address the author delivered on April 27, 1992, before an audience of faculty and students from the nine member schools of the Boston Theological Institute (BTI) who had gathered at the Museum of Science for a program entitled "The Renewal of Reverence: Theological Education in the Environmental Era." Massie spoke following a special showing of the film,* The Blue Planet.]

In June of 1991, when I first saw *The Blue Planet* at the meeting of the Joint Appeal in Religion and Science, it affected me deeply. I am not an environmental scientist or a theologian. I am an Episcopal priest who studies economic questions. Yet when I saw the film, I immediately thought of passages from the book of Genesis. God, having labored to bring the world into being, having set it spinning on its course, takes a few steps back, looks, and is overcome by the beauty of that Creation: "And God saw that it was very good."

For thousands of years, human beings have wanted to do the same, to step back for a moment and look at the whole world at once. You and I, unlike our parents and grandparents and all of the generations who have gone before us, have the chance to do just that. Through our technology, we can now step back and gaze at our home, with its swirling clouds, its flashes of nighttime lightning, its blue waters.

Through the same science and technology, we have increased our power as a species at an unimaginable rate. We all know that our ability to adjust morally, politically, and spiritually to our new-found strength has been severely tested. It is a tragedy that humanity, having just witnessed the longed-for reduction of the nuclear threat, must now emerge to face an even more serious menace. It is more serious because the symptoms have developed so slowly and because the instruments of destruction are not fearsome weapons lying in hardened silos but friendly appliances humming in our kitchens and garages.

Yet the repercussions of human activity on our planet's integrity grow more dangerous with each passing moment. Every day, silently, without fanfare, the flimsy gaseous membrane floating miles above our heads is shredded by hundreds of tons of human-made chemicals. Every day, silently, without fanfare, another four hundred thousand babies arrive on this Earth yearning for food, for shelter, and for a decent life. Every day, silently, without fanfare, the atmospheric temperature rises a tiny fraction, unleashing bizarre and destructive weather patterns and moving us even closer to massive natural disruptions.

Why have we not acted?

Scientists have known about these trends for more than a decade, and they have become increasingly alarmed. Despite their concern, they have been ignored by our government, and they have been ignored by our churches. And the question we must answer is this: Why have we not heeded their warnings?

1. We have been busy with other matters.

Let me try to answer with a story. Recently, I went to Toronto, where I spent the weekend with a religious community called L'Arche. At L'Arche, able-bodied persons live in community with severely disabled persons as a witness to Christian love. It is a marvelous place, filled with the spirit of God. I stayed on the third floor of one of their houses. When I went into the bathroom, I noticed that the faucet was dripping. I could tell that it had been dripping for months or even for years, because where the water struck the sink, all the enamel had been worn away. There was a large ugly black circle of cast-iron, which was rusting without its protective coating.

I put a container under the drip to measure how much water was passing through. The leak filled a cup every three minutes. That's five quarts an hour. That meant that every day they were losing thirty gallons of fresh spring water which they pumped from an underwater aquifer. Over a year they had lost eleven thousand gallons down the drain: drip, drip, drip.

This, to me, became a symbol of the problems of the Church with regard to the environment. The L'Arche community was distracted by their central responsibilities. They did not notice the loss of water because it was in a small bathroom, out of sight. Apparently, none of the other guests had brought it to the residents' attention, each guest probably thinking that it was someone else's responsibility. Or perhaps the members of the community had noticed it, but doubted that a few drips of water could be the sign of a serious problem. Being ethereal religious types, they may have considered the idea of going to the hardware store and buying a wrench and a washer too technical, or hiring a plumber too expensive. But their inattention led to waste and destruction.

I think there are many lessons in this for us. The churches and the seminaries have not paid close attention to these questions because we have been distracted. The churches have been busy for decades on behalf of civil rights, human rights, nuclear war, and economic justice. We have done this in addition to our more conventional but equally compelling responsiblities to examine, reform, and convey the Christian tradition and to minister to the emotional and spiritual injuries that rend individual human lives.

Even when the churches have been able to seize a few reflective moments from our unrelenting daily demands, our intellectual attention has been captured by other critical quesitons, questions of sexuality, gender, and race; questions of authority, tradition, and hierarchy. All these questions have been, and remain, vital. And they are interrelated. Together they form the prologue for the greatest challenge humans have ever faced, that of working together to avert the tragedy to which our behavior has destined us. In the words of the Joint Appeal in Religion and Science, "In this challenge lies the opportunity for people of faith to affirm and enact, at a scale as never before, what it truly means to be religious."

2. We have fallen into the breach between religion and science.

A second reason for our lethargic response has been the historical breach between religion and science. The breach has been based on the fear in both communities of mutual contamination, on a long history of misunderstanding and intolerance, and on the different personalities the fields attract.

But we have been too quick to use this breach to cover up our shortcomings and insecurities. Too many who pursue vocations as clergy or as seminary faculty cloak their unwillingness or incapacity to think numerically with the contention that numbers are irrelevant or evil. Too many who pursue vocations in the sciences cloak their unwillingness or incapacity to acknowledge the values shaping their decisions with the contention that scientific methods and outcomes are value-free.

For a long time, this breach was merely childish. Now it is becoming dangerous. Some scientists, to their great credit, have realized that information alone does not change behavior. They have begun reaching out to the religious community, through the Joint Appeal in New York or the Center for Faith and Science Exchange at the Boston Theological Institute. Even someone like Carl Sagan, who describes himself as a "confirmed skeptic with regard to matters of revealed truth," has understood that scientific information must be linked to the elemental moral and religious traditions of our culture if they are to have force. A central challenge for us, then, as the stewards and critics of those moral and religious traditions, is whether we will have the courage to respond.

3. We have been in denial.

There is a third possible reason for our inaction. Perhaps we have intuitively grasped the magnitude of the problem but have been in denial, like a woman I once knew when I was a hospital chaplain who refused to go to chemotherapy because she refused to admit she had cancer. What she really feared, I think, was the loss of hope in the face of a personal apocalypse.

We are all like that to some degree. The more we consider the magnitude of the possible devastation of the whole planet, the more paralyzed we become by fatalistic terror. We are like small animals, frozen in the middle of the road by the headlights of an oncoming Mack truck.

What are the dangers of inaction?

1. Confrontation with neopaganism and Social Darwinism

To some readers my words may seem inappropriate. You may believe that it is not the responsibility of the churches or of seminaries to explore matters of science, economics, and public policy. You may believe that it is even dangerous for the Christian Church to dilute the message of the Gospel of Jesus Christ with the gauzy creed of some modern environmentalists

Yet I believe that the theological danger of remaining apart is far greater than that of becoming engaged. If the churches of Jesus Christ refuse to acknowedge the new global and scientific realities, if the churches of Jesus Christ refuse to articulate a persuasive commitment to care for our world, then hundreds of millions of persons who are yearning for spiritual leadership will be forced by our arrogant inertia to look elsewhere.

I will not presume to say how the rich biblical traditions of Creation and redemption should be recalibrated and interpreted by our nation's diverse religious communities in light of the unfolding environmental cataclysm. But I will say that every community of faith must seek those new interpretations, because there are serious moral problems in the romantic neopaganism or the incipient Social Darwinism which sometimes wafts through the environmental movement.

The romantic temptation to view nature as a perfectly balanced, inherently sacred, and intrinsically happy place, a Garden of Eden before its desecration by humans, is a picture which, beneath its attractive surface, conceals an ethic of cruelty. Nature may be balanced, but it is an equlibrium of death. Most creatures spend their lives trying to avoid being violently captured, dismembered, and consumed.

Similarly, under the iron morality of Darwinism, the poor and the weak of other species are viewed as parasites who deserve to be eaten. The temptation to take such models of nature and to use them as the normative code for humanity is strong. One need only look at how Social Darwinism, using nature as its guide, has repeatedly justified the oppression or destruction of whole populations of human beings to glimpse the calamities of such a course.

2. Confrontation with economics

There are other dangers to our silence and inaction. The functional illiteracy of most seminary students and faculty with regard to economics, the central form of political discourse in our world, means that we cannot gauge the strengths and weaknesses of the claims being made in its name. Because we do not understand the strengths of market theory, we cannot affirm efforts like Project 88 at the Harvard Kennedy School of Government which is attempting to find ways to make polluters pay for their pollution.

Nor, unhappily, can we react to the stream of statements made by economists on matters that shape our future. For example, in June 1991, a professor of economics from the University of Chicago named Gary Becker wrote a column for *Business Week* in which he denounced proposals to lower CO_2 emissions as ridiculous and extreme.

He writes: "Any likely amount of warming will probably have minor effects on manufacturing, mining, transportation, finance, and most other services. . . [S]ome crops would suffer from too much heat and dryness, countries with warm climates would get less comfortable, and in extreme cases, some coastal regions would be flooded by melting glaciers. On the other hand, warming would presumably benefit cold climates such as Canada's and encourage farming in high-latitude regions."

Notice how Becker uses the language of probability to hedge his attack: "Any likely amount of warming will probably have minor effects." Yet what if Becker is wrong? Will we accept his home as collateral when millions of residents of coastal cities find their homes destroyed and throng to our doors? Will we be satisfied with his apology if all the microorganisms in the ocean suddenly die because of an overdose of ultraviolet light, wiping out the entire ocean food chain?

Or take another example. According to the *Boston Globe,* on March 8, 1992, William Nordhaus, a professor of economics at Yale, told the Massachusetts Department of Public Utilities in a hearing that, "The current generation should not make large sacrifices to slow climate change today if future generations are richer and can slow climate change themselves." Leave it to our children, he is saying, to pay the tab in blood.

These people are not crackpots. They are the high priests of the prevailing secular religion in America. They are presenting us with a possible future in which billions of human beings will be forced to migrate thousands of miles to seek shelter from the sky and to compete even more violently than we already do for basic resources, and they are presenting this possibility as a rational, reasonable, morally acceptable risk. What they are really saying is that we as a society should not give up playing Russian roulette because we are having such a good time, because it would be inconvenient to stop now, and because we really do not know exactly how many bullets are in the chamber.

This is not just stupid, it is immoral. The gun, when it goes off, will not slay the privileged or the powerful. The professors of economics and of theology will continue to argue and to eat. The gun, when it goes off, as it already has, kills the voiceless and the defenseless first.

This is a direct challenge to every human being with moral sensibilities and especially to those with religious commitments. The willingness of our modern leaders and of our culture to sacrifice future generations on the altar of our own consumerist greed is in direct contradiction to the biblical requirement for stewardship.

Yet it goes on, protested by only a few squeaks from the picket line or a few squawks from the pulpit. Even as you read this, business interests in the United States and in other industrialized countries are attempting to use international free-trade agreements to eviscerate national environmental regulations. The president and vice president of the United States, instead of facing up to their immense and unique responsibilities, have effectively undermined every attempt to rein in this corporate juggernaut.

Some environmentalists and scientists have objected, but those who inhabit the churches and the seminaries, with the exception of a few remarkable visionaries, have been largely mute. We have been cowed into silence by our inferiority complexes, distracted by our internal conflicts, and shackled by our relentless desire to be liked. I have been in the sanctuaries, and I have been in the classrooms, and what I see more than anything else is timidity.

In the Second Letter to Timothy we are reminded that, "The spirit that God gave us is no craven spirit, but one to inspire strength, love, and self-discipline." We are supposed to beam with the light of hope and resurrection, a lamp on the lamppost testifying to the power of life over destruction and despair.

There are a few hopeful signs. Some denominations have passed resolutions and formed committees to explore environmental initiatives. Others, like the Lutherans and Presbyterians, have produced study guides for local churches, though I feel those have largely been ignored. A few seminaries have made preliminary steps in the direction of recycling or in tentatively permitting new courses and new discussions.

I am proud that Harvard Divinity School, for example, has established the Harvard Seminar on Environmental Values, directed by Timothy C. Weiskel. It has funded a field placement at the school for a student environment minister, has supported new ideas like linking churches to community farms, and was able through the splendid work of a group of dedicated students, faculty, and staff volunteers to put this forum together.

These things are not enough. We may recycle our paper, but we are not yet willing to compost our food. We may evaluate the companies from whom we purchase, but we are not yet willing to look at those in whom we invest. We may be willing to offer elective courses on environmental issues, but we are not yet willing to live them from our hearts.

It is in those values that we will find the key to the great collective action problem we face. Just as the game between persons who refuse to cheat will be different from one played by those who want to win at all costs, so will a world in which the dominant citizens actively consider the well-being of the planet be different from one dominated by the Darwinian exploitation of the poor for the benefit of the rich. The only comprehensive solution to the environmental crisis will be to establish, model, and proclaim a shift in our values towards the world, a shift toward justice.

Such a shift of values is not going to come from the White House, from Congress, from the State House, from television, from the laboratory, from the public schools, or from the Boston Museum of Science. It is not going to come from the departments of philosophy, history, or psychology. It is not going to come from the law, business, or medical schools.

Each of the groups I have mentioned does propagate values and may be working on environmental questions, but not a single one of them has as its explicit purpose, its mission, the teaching about the most important values in life. In society's views, and in our own, it is the seminaries who have the primary responsibility to ponder humanity's most profound spiritual truths. The responsibility thus lies not exclusively but principally with us.

A hundred years from now, in a world groaning under the weight of twelve billion hungry bodies, in a world where children play at night to avoid the searing sun, in a world filled with museums displaying pictures of plants, animals, forests, and lakes that no longer exist, future historians, ethicists, and theologians will look back to our day.

What will they see? Will they wring their hands mournfully when they see that we were too concerned with minutiae and bickering to see the sky dissipating above our heads? If we so readily condemn the privileged citizens of prewar Germany for ignoring the warning signs of devastation, for refusing to speak and act while there was still time, how can we escape a similar judgment from our offspring?

Will the historians of the future shake their heads in regret and disbelief that we, who had a chance, squandered it in hesitancy? Or will they write doctoral dissertations about the bold beginning of the "Boston Movement," when men and women of faith rose above their circumstances, and above their self-interest, and unleashed a whirlwind of change?

The choice of what they write is ours. We can no longer doze beneath the sleepy comforter of denial. We have cancer. We need chemotherapy. We must face up to the truth of the oncoming climate change and reflect on the implications of that change for our work, our future, and for those for whom we are responsible.

You may feel uneasy with this. Perhaps you think that you already have too many responsibilities, that you already are as committed as you can be, and that, besides, you are not the most talented person available. If you feel the call is untimely, unfair, or inappropriately directed, I would like to remind you of the great traditon in which you stand. Abraham was reluctant to depart from Ur for the land of Canaan, Moses was reluctant to return to Egypt and confront Pharaoah, Isaiah and Jeremiah were reluctant to accept their prophetic responsibilities, Esther was reluctant to defend her people before the king, Jonah was reluctant to preach repentance to the people of Nineveh, and Peter was reluctant to leave his nets. At every moment, from every one of the one hundred human generations which stretch from Moses until today, God has called the imperfect, the uncertain, and the unworthy at inappropriate times to do the impossible.

In our own day we are fascinated by the confluence of history and character which caused Oscar Romero, Mohandas Gandhi, Martin Luther King, Jr., Mother Teresa, and the many other unnamed and unrecognized heroes to engage and transform their circumstances. In our seminary classes, these figures dance around the room, revered as saints who faced historic challenges. The time has come to stop dreaming about the days of old. The call has now come to us.

In the name of the life-giving forests, the bountiful sea, the wide and wounded sky; in the name of the millions of God's creatures who have no human voice but who cry for assistance; and in the name of the God who has given us life, freed us from the bonds of judgment, and charged us to be stewards of all Creation, I ask you, I urge you, to join us and to change the course of our global destiny.

April 27, 1992

The SecuLar City and the SacRed EaRth

TIMOTHY C. WEISKEL

We are in big trouble. Truly terrifying trouble. Trouble from which—on our own—it is not likely that we will ever fully recover. Organized religion and professional theologians are in part to blame for accentuating the problems we face. Yet we cannot simply dismiss the theologians and dispense with religion. On the contrary, we need both more than ever. It is only through a fundamental reformulation of our religiously held beliefs and a thorough transformation of our public theology that we—the entire human species—will have any realistic chance of long-term survival in the twenty-first century or beyond.

For a variety of reasons—some of them apparently related to our religious beliefs, humans remain fundamentally ignorant of or collectively indifferent toward the fate of other species, insisting instead that measurements of human welfare should be the only criteria governing human behavior. Yet it is upon the enduring presence of other life-forms and the integrity of system-wide functions they perform that human survival depends. Thus, we live in the midst of an unresolved but rapidly escalating ecological paradox. In evolutionary and historical terms we are too successful for our own good. We refashion the natural world to suit our perceived needs and wants, yet—to date—these anthropogenic microcosms have proved to be ecologically unsustainable and in the long run collectively suicidal for human welfare. It seems as if humankind is at war with the natural world. The good news and the bad news is that we are winning. The tragedy is that by winning, we lose. Without some strong and governing principle of limit, we are likely to lose in a big way.

Literary scholars and documentary historians have long regarded the rise and fall of cities and civilizations as largely a manifestation of particular ideas, organizing principles, or religious beliefs. Now it is possible to decipher the record of archaeological sites to learn substantially more about the ecological dynamics of decline than were ever recorded in sacred or secular texts.

The new evidence is not encouraging. The history of cities has been associated with the history of repeated ecological disaster. The growth of cities and social and military conflict both manifest and exacerbate this dynamic of environmental decline. C. S. Lewis's observation has proved sadly correct, that "the so-called struggle of man against nature is really a struggle of man against man with nature as an instrument."

This kind of ecological characterization of the city does not sound very balanced or appreciative. At the very least, it seems to ignore the technological capacities of humans to improve their environments. After all, it could be argued, the development of cities has been synonymous with the growth of civilization, science, the arts, and humane learning. Surely these aspects of the human story are net positive achievements that have permanently improved human welfare. But in extolling the liberating virtues of the modern city we have mistaken our privileged and limited experience for that of humankind in general.

What does any of this have to do with religion? A great deal. I am convinced that the central locus of religious concern in the coming century will be the irreducible tension between the secular city and the sacred Earth—between the world of human artifice and technological achievement on the one hand and the natural bio-geo-chemical processes that sustain us within the natural world on the other hand. The central task of contemporary religious thinkers should be to help humanity come to terms with the fact of the secular city, for there simply is no going back, no realistic hope of recreating a preurban past.

Radical principles of self-imposed self-restraint will be required if we are to survive the urban circumstances of our own creation. In the past, religious communities have been the locus for the full elaboration of ethical principles of restraint and for a sense of awe and reverence for the entirity of Creation and our miraculous appearance within it. It is to these faith communities and their core beliefs in the awe-inspiring, sacred otherness of 0 that we need now to turn again.

All theological systems involve the elaboration of particular principles of personal empowerment and human limit. Rather than simply dismissing these kinds of reflections as superfluous in our day, we ought to be redoubling our thought and work on these themes. The task is far more than an academic exercise. It will need to become the substance of the core beliefs that control our conscious and unconscious behavior. Without a compelling image of human limit guiding our decisions in the coming years and decades, we are likely to drive ourselves—and a great many other species as well—into a syndrome of accelerated extinction.

But this extinction event will be like none previously recorded. It will be the first one generated by species arrogance and, thus, the first one engendered by the failure of theology. If theology is essentially a theory of human limit, then it can only be through a rapid and thorough reformulation of this kind of thinking that we will be able to avoid what seems to be in store for us.

There is an old Chinese proverb that states simply, "If you do not change direction, you will probably end up where you are going." That is a chilling thought for us, as it was, no doubt, for Isaiah, too, when he wrote: ". . . the heavens grow thin like smoke, the Earth wears out like a garment, and its inhabitants die like flies. . . ." (Isa. 51:6).

✦ II ✦
A NEW, NEW WORLD

The Earth Our Kin

MARY CATHERINE BATESON

I heard an address at the Lindisfarne Association several years ago, by a Tibetan abbot, on the meditation called "The Recognition of the Mother," which was supposed to teach people how to discover compassion. One reflects that the world has existed from all eternity through countless cycles of reincarnation and that therefore all other sentient beings have no doubt in some incarnation at some point in infinite time been one's mother. Reflecting on that, one discovers compassion for them. The good abbot paused, with a puzzled frown, while the translator caught up with him, and he said "You know, that just doesn't seem to speak to Americans. They may not feel quite the same way about their mothers, so I tell Americans, 'Try to meditate on the recognition of the best friend.'"

People acquire their ability to receive and to give love from their early family experiences. And in most cultures the metaphors and patterns of thought that are used to teach ethical treatment of people outside the family are metaphors through the system of kinship. We heard something of this in the Gospel this morning—that the peacemakers are the sons of God. We speak of ourselves as children of God and hope that this will allow us to deal more gently with each other.

But kinship systems change. When people want to take the close relationships of the family, in the form that they take in that culture, and extend them to include a larger group, they will be using patterns which differ from place to place and from time to time. Perhaps, as in the tradition in which we are speaking this morning, kinship is reckoned by descent through the male line, so we see ourselves as kin because we believe we have the same father. In other places the important link may be through the female line.

There are many different systems for taking the small immediate experience of intimacy and extending it metaphorically. One of the images that is used is the image of Earth as our mother. It is an unfortunate image in many ways at the present state of this civilization. People leave their mothers. Mothers get worn out and put on the shelf. Spaceships are launched, casting off umbilical ties to the planet. And the metaphors of Earth as our mother tend—in the way in which, I am afraid, we are treating mothers and fathers in this civilization—tend to encourage our resignation to the wearing out and using up of the wealth of this planet.

People also need images based on kinship to think about time. They need them to think horizontally about their relationships to people in the present—strangers, new people—and they also need notions of kinship to think about their relationships to the past and to the future. We seem to be at a point in time where we are profoundly unable to place what we do in relation to the past and future. We live with the extraordinary image of ourselves planning within one or two generations to exhaust resources that took millennia to create: energy resources, oil especially, using up the past. And look how this is almost symmetrically reflected in the way in which we are now likely to preempt the future. The substances created through time in the past will be exhausted, and we in turn will create substances such as radioactive wastes that will be with the planet equal millennia into the future, endangering all life.

We are in urgent need of new ways of experiencing these problems, and I do think that the metaphors of kinship are the place to start to find metaphors for thinking about time and relationships. But I think we need to change the form in which we are using these metaphors. Of course, we can go on speaking like St. Francis of our Brother Sun, Sister Moon, Earth Our Mother, above all God Our Father, but we need to incorporate a changing sense of family and relationship so that the metaphors don't do more harm than good.

I would like to suggest to you another meditation, if you like. I think each person trying to decide in this period how to live, what action to take, where to set their thermostats, how often to drive their automobiles, whom to vote for, what to do with their Coca-Cola bottles—I believe each person needs to be sure that they have in their own lives a relationship with at least one real flesh-and-blood child. There are a great many people whose children have grown up and moved to other cities, who do not have relationships with children in their lives, and increasing numbers of adults who do not plan to have children. Furthermore, I think we must expect an increasing number of people to want to push children they already have out of their lives, to repudiate contact with children, to raise the question of whether parents shouldn't be able to decide, later on, that dealing with children is a burden that they don't want to continue to bear. There are a lot of reasons for this.

One reason, I think, why many people prefer not to have children in their lives, is that we are today living at the expense of children. What we use and what we waste will not be there for them, and the pollution we create will be. It is not surprising that if people feel, at some deep level, that their style of life is lived at the expense of the future, that they will not want reminders of the future around them. At the same time I think we have made a fundamental mistake in thinking that children are raised by parents. Parents are essential, but no two people can raise a child. Much less, one-and-a-half people or two halves. We should think of child rearing as we think about the growth of organisms now, including the realization of how complexly structured the nutrients they must have are; how much pattern there must be in the environment to make life and growth possible; how much diversity and stimulation and love from many people a child needs to mature. What we are realizing essentially is that the environment a child needs to grow in—sometimes it is referred to as "normal expectable environment"—is one of the great and complex miracles.

This environment is a vast collaboration, a dance of co-parenting by air and water and Sun and Moon and living creatures and bacteria and plants and other people. I suggest that we need to involve each of our lives with the life of at least one child so that that child will not be isolated, restrained, and overburdened. So that every child will have as many concerned adults as possible. And so that we, looking at that child, can reflect on the vast network needed to give that child a future. I know what I want my child to have. I want her to have the pleasure that I have in her, from another child sometime in the future. And I see it going ahead. I want the life to continue there, beyond my immediate imagination. And then we can build up in our imagination the sense of the other human beings and the natural forces interlocked in care for that child.

It is not enough that we look at each other and say we are brothers and sisters. To say we are brothers and sisters is a way of saying that we come from a common past, we have a certain similarity that binds us to each other. I think we need to look at each other, at the planet, at the natural forces around us, and say, "My love, my bridegroom, my bride." Together we will be parents. We will become kin to each other and treat each other with love, because out of our differences and out of our diversity comes the future. We will knit ourselves to each other by metaphors of kinship, in common nurturance of the ongoing life of this planet. And as we realize how many must be engaged with us in that parenthood, how broad is the communion and interrelationship that makes that life possible, then we find that we are indeed encompassed about by a "host of witnesses." And that it is that makes faith possible.

Amen.

November 4, 1979

Responsible
to Creation

AL GORE, JR.

May I say by way of disclaimer, since I am in the profession of politics, that I deeply respect and honor the tradition in our country, learned from hard experience, to separate government and religion. May I ask your indulgence to allow me to speak here as an individual even as I respect that tradition.

I have been here before and may I pay honor to those who have made this the Green Cathedral, the environmental Cathedral, a place where prophecy is heard and has been for a long time. Early prophetic sermons in the 1970s were preached here by Buckminster Fuller, Margaret Mead, Gregory Bateson, Thomas Berry, James Lovelock; and under the leadership of Dean Morton and others, the Cathedral has become one of New York's first recycling centers and has developed a greenhouse bioshelter with, among other things, a project to develop soil for rooftop gardens. It is a think-tank for restoration ecology, and the list of contributions goes on and on.

But may I mention just one other specifically. I was here earlier this year at a rather extraordinary meeting that was purposely held outside the view of the news media so that people might be willing to change during the conversations that took place. It was a meeting called the Joint Appeal with denominational leaders from a broad range of religions and denominations, gathering together with scientists to examine the problems now besetting the global environment. At the conclusion of those discussions the religious leaders issued a joint statement which said, and I quote, "We believe a consensus now exists at the highest level of leadership across a significant spectrum of religious traditions, that the cause of environmental integrity and justice must occupy a position of utmost priority for people of faith."

People of faith indeed will make the crucial difference in determining whether or not our civilization is successful in confronting the extraordinary crisis we now face. At the heart of the problem is our relationship to the Earth. This [St. Francis Day] service, now in its seventh year, is remarkable in part because it celebrates the reawakening of a truer expression of what our relationship to the other living things of the Earth really is.

When God made his covenant with Noah and gave the rainbow as a symbol of his promise, he went on to make another covenant expressed in the very next verse, a covenant with all living things and the entire Earth. What is our relationship to all living things and the entire Earth? The purpose of life I was taught in Sunday School many years ago is to glorify God. If we heap contempt upon God's Creation, what does that say about our relationship to God? Our relationship to Creation is therefore critical in expressing our relationship to God.

Where is God? Where is Heaven? *Where* is a word which refers to a physical place. I recently spoke to a group of elementary school students and asked that question. I asked many of them if they would point to the location of Heaven. And you know, of course, where they pointed: they pointed straight up. We have all of us absorbed the notion that God is way out there, somewhere, perhaps an old man with a white beard, living far from the Earth. Where is Hell? We've been taught to point straight down to the center of the Earth. But Jesus told us that the Kingdom of God is within. Is God in us? Why are so many uncomfortable with that notion? And if God is within us, is God not also within other living things? Is God not also in the rest of Creation?

Early in the history of Christianity the message of Christ was wrapped tightly in the language and metaphors of Greek philosophy, a rich tradition from which we selected some things and left out others. In the process we understood some of Christ's message, and we set aside other parts. The Church faced an existing body of religious beliefs in much of the world in which the gospel was preached. Paganism and animism derived a revelation from the physical world. Some believed that in each separate individual animal and plant and rock there was a separate motivating spirit. In the desire to overcome this superstitious way of relating to the world, our tradition placed heavy emphasis on a disembodied spirit which we worshipped intellectually.

A moment ago the Word was held up supreme and triumphant, a Word which we received intellectually and understand intellectually. We can also feel the presence of God. We can also understand God emotionally and physically and receive a revelation from all of the world. We are not separate from the Earth. God is not separate from the Earth.

One of the windows in a bay several columns back celebrates technology, and a window portrays the technology of television when it was first used here in this city back in the 1920s. All the new technologies we have used have convinced us that we can employ our intellect to completely understand the world, to master it, to manipulate it, to do with it as we wish. Now we have acquired new technologies and new powers, and the scale of humankind's existence on the Earth is out of all proportion to what it has been throughout all of human history up until now.

I talked with some scientists recently about a new technology which if it had existed at the time this window was created would be portrayed there, the technology called holograms. Bear with me just for a moment, because I think it is interesting as a metaphor. I don't pretend to understand it, but perhaps you have seen these apparent three-dimensional images which sometimes seem to—well, they're on Mastercards and Visas, and other kinds can be placed in a room where they seem to float as a three-dimensional image. How do they work? I don't know, but I wish to describe one characteristic which is of special interest. Because of the unique laws of optics, every tiny part of the hologram screen has the entire three-dimensional image very faintly represented. When the full screen is brought into view, then a large image becomes visible.

It seems to me that God's relationship to Creation as we perceive it is not unlike that phenomenon. I believe that God is visible and perceptible in every corner of Creation, but to our senses only faintly. Only when we can envision in our mind's eye and in our hearts the fullness of God's Creation can we see vividly the image of God.

We are taught that we have dominion over this Creation, but we also know full well that we are stewards of this Creation, and we share a very special responsibility for preserving it and for protecting it. In three of the Gospels, those of Matthew, Mark, and Luke, there is the parable of the unfaithful servant, wherein the master instructs his servant, upon leaving for a journey, that he must take care of the house, and he gives one very simple rule. If, while I'm gone, he says, vandals come and ransack this house, or thieves come to steal my belongings, it will not be a good enough excuse if you tell me you were asleep.

We are now witnessing in our lifetimes environmental vandalism in God's home on a global scale. One-and-a-half acres of rain forest are lost per second. All the recent oil well fires in Kuwait put together represent only one percent of the pollution we put into the atmosphere every day worldwide. The destruction of living species is so rapid that within the lifetimes of young people here in this Cathedral, we could— unless we stop it —witness the loss of more than half of all the living creatures God put on Earth.

It will not be good enough for us to say we were asleep. It is an insufficient excuse for us to claim we were unaware of what is going on in God's home right now. We have an obligation to act, first of all in our own lives, and then in our own community, in our nation, and in our world. We have an obligation to those who are less fortunate. We have an obligation to social justice, and we have an obligation to protect this Earth against the rapacious destruction now underway.

Is there hope that we can succeed in this task? Those of us gathered here who are believers believe in a God of hope, a God of miracles, a God who promises us that we can have a future completely outside the boundaries of our own imagination, that what comes in the future need not be what has come in the past, and that we have a responsibility to co-create that future.

In Revelations, John says we will praise the lamb triumphant with all creatures. And we are told the Earth is the Lord's and the fullness thereof. Let us when we leave this place take the feeling of joy which we are experiencing here and join with it a commitment to pray, to act, to change, and to protect God's Creation.

Biosphere as
a Single Organism

JAMES E. LOVELOCK

I do not share the view fashionable in some quarters that the exploration of space is wasteful of the Earth's resources and extravagant at a time when so many in the world are poor and in need. For me, those voyages into space have given a new view of our planetary home. Not just that of a glorious azure globe which now is almost a visual cliché, but rather something new in the mind's eye, just as the unexpected bonus of a vacation is the way it returns us to the familiar home scene in a new and pleasant way.

Revelations about the Earth seen from space are not limited to the wonder in the minds of astronauts nor to our sharing it vicariously with them through the images seen on our television screens. The Earth has also been seen from outside by the more discerning eyes of scientific instruments, and these have shown our planet to be extraordinary and unique in the solar system. Although the Earth is made of the same elements and in similar proportions as are Mars and Venus, it is as different from these its sister planets as is a man or a tree different from a pillar of rock.

There is nothing unusual about the idea of the life on Earth interacting with the air, seas, and rocks, but it took a view from outside to glimpse the possibility that all of these together, the air, the ocean, the soil, and all living things, may constitute a single, giant living system and one with the capacity to keep the Earth always at a state most favorable for the life upon it.

In such a context, the air we breathe is not just a part of the environment; it is a part of life itself. To put it another way, it is as if the air was to the biosphere as is the fur to a cat or the paper to a hornet's nest—not living but a purposeful product of living things made specifically to protect against an otherwise hostile environment. For the Earth itself, the air protects against the rigors of space.

Now an entity comprising a whole planet with the powerful capacity to regulate its climate and its chemical composition needs a name to match. I was fortunate in having as a near neighbor in our village, the novelist William Golding. When I discussed this notion with him during a walk, he proposed the name Gaia, which the early Greeks used for the Earth. I was glad, for scientists like to quote the first literate civilization, and, moreover, it was a simple four-letter word. Its use forestalled the birth of ear-grating acronyms based on ugly phrases like biogeochemical cybernetic cycles. Whenever henceforward I talk of Gaia, I mean it as shorthand for the hypothetical entity with the capacity to homeostat the Earth.

The Gaia Hypothesis is still unproven, but as is often the way in science, this is less important than is its use as a kind of refracting glass through which to see the world differently. The concept is an aid in the formulation of new questions to ask about the Earth.

I do not propose to take long in arguing the scientific evidence for Gaia. But I will use two illustrative pieces of evidence so that you can see that it is more than just a flight of fancy.

Firstly, throughout the long history of life on Earth (three and a half billion years) the climate has never differed much from what it is now. To be sure, there have been ice ages, but, contrary to common belief, these are limited in effect to the outer parts of the north and south temperate regions and do not greatly affect the whole climate. What points to Gaia is that during this same long period, our source of heat—that great radiator, the Sun—has increased its output by at least one third. If the temperature on Earth was right in the beginning, why do we not now boil? It is difficult to demonstrate that equable temperature could have so long been maintained without some process of regulation.

Then there is the matter of oxygen. Although we and other animals would soon die without it, oxygen has not always been present in the air.

One-fifth of the air is now oxygen. We can ask, would it matter if one quarter of the air were oxygen, instead of one fifth? For breathing, we couldn't tell the difference. But at one quarter, that is twenty-five per cent, so great would be the increase in flammability that a single flash of lightning would be sufficient to ignite even the damp tropical rain forests and cause them and almost all of the standing vegetation to burn away in a vast conflagration. Thus, it seems that both the climate and the composition of the air are regulated so as to be favorable for life.

These are just two of the scientific arguments for Gaia. But if I presented all of them, it would only corroborate (not prove) her existence. But there is enough, I think, to justify us in considering what difference her possible presence can make for us and for our relationships with all of the other living things on Earth.

If we are "all creatures great and small" a part of Gaia, from microorganisms to whales, then we are all of us potentially important to her well-being. The ecologists' warning about the undesirability of eliminating species takes on a new significance. No longer can we merely regret the passing of one of the great whales, or the blue butterfly, or even, conceivably, the smallpox virus. When one of these is eliminated from the Earth, perhaps in the careless pursuit of our own selfish interests, we may, if Gaia exists, have destroyed a part of ourselves, for we also are a part of Gaia.

There are as many possibilities for comfort as there are for dismay in contemplating the consequences of our membership in this great democracy of living things. For example, it might be that one role we play is as the senses and nervous system for Gaia. Through our eyes, she has for the first time seen her very fair face and in our minds has become aware of herself in a conscious sense.

Moreover, we can reason and anticipate on her behalf as well as on ours, and therefore perhaps at some future date we may need to use our vast powers to protect against some danger whether it be internal, as from our own pollutions, or external, as from an imminent ice age.

Then, there may be nothing unusual in the possibility that natural selection has in us, as well as in other animals, led to the development of a sense of pleasure in the presence of beauty. Could it be that the pleasures we feel at the sight of a sweet and seemly landscape are part of a natural reward for keeping things right? And in a complementary way, the pain suffered at the sight of a degraded and derelict natural scene might be due punishment for our neglect or destructiveness.

Nearly all of us in the Western world are urbanized. We live in cities, suburbs, or exurbs, and as a consequence, we are all of us cut off from nature. The brief contact experienced during vacations hardly counts. Because of this alienation from the natural world forced upon us by our way of life, it is more than ever necessary to have a better understanding of the world outside the city, if we are to live in harmony with Gaia.

It is usual to regard the place where we live as the center of the world. If this happens to be a large city like New York, London, or Tokyo, inevitably the environment reflects the imbalance between people and their artifacts like cars, and other living things. Such an environment is almost certain to be polluted, and therefore we tend to think wrongly that the whole world also is polluted. But cities make up only a tiny fraction of the Earth's surface, and air pollution, although important to those who dwell in them, has a negligible effect on the rest of the biosphere. What we do in our cities matters nothing like so much as what happens in the hinterland, where few are present to see it. In such places, there may be local overfarming, or in more distant places, the potentially more danger-ous wholesale destruction of tropical forest ecosystems, to say nothing of the grossly improvident overfishing of the oceans.

Shakespeare was able to write in *A Midsummer Night's Dream* of a "Bank whereon the wild thyme blew, where oxlips and the nodding vio-let grew." Were he alive today, it would take him more than an hour to travel from the Globe Theatre to the nearest countryside. There, he would find that the banks where the thyme grew had vanished along with the oxlips and with nearly all of the violets.

Rachael Carson in her famous book, *The Silent Spring*, predicted such a change in the countryside, and in many parts of England it has come about. But it has not happened in the way she thought it would, from the cumulative poisoning effect of pesticides and of other agricultural chem-icals. In fact, the change has taken place because of our demands for food. The farmer is now obliged to regard all living things other than his crops, livestock, family, and hired help as either weeds, pests, or vermin. He regards it as his duty to destroy them by any means he can find. I might add that I have not noticed that organic farmers are very different from the others in this respect. Now, the modern farmer does his job very well indeed, so it is not surprising that fewer and fewer places are left for the song birds to rear their young. Indeed, very many of the plants and animals that were the joy of our countryside only twenty years ago, are now extinct. It is quite wrong to blame pesticides and pollution for this adverse change. It makes no more sense to do so than it would to blame the axe-maker or the axe for Lizzie Bordon's fit of homicide. It is the sheer weight of our numbers which has made it happen.

Grandfathers tend to regard all change as malign and to say that things were better in the past. In fact no one really knows whether or not these changes in the natural world are harmful or benign. It may be that we shall, as René Dubos observed, come to regard what now seems to be the ugly face of agribusiness as pleasant in itself. Future generations may look upon vast green expanses of perfect weed-free grain undulating in the breeze as beautiful—like some inland ocean.

We ought to be able to live with Gaia at many different population densities and in many different ways. If it should turn out that the most important regions of the Earth for homeostasis are the continental shelves of the oceans, then we might be able to farm the land surfaces with some kind of impunity.

But if Gaia does indeed exist, and especially if the land surfaces include vital parts of her system, then we should consider the consequences. If our numbers, together with the even larger numbers of our dependent species, which includes not only crops and farm animals but also opportunitistic species like rats and seagulls and many others who grow with us, if we and all of these others continue to grow in numbers, then at some time, whether through wastefulness or by the sheer pressure of numbers, we shall stifle Gaia. If that happens, then we may find ourselves to be conscripted for life-long service in the corps of planetary maintenance engineers. We shall no longer be travelers on a living planet but slaves aboard that prison hulk, the spaceship Earth. And then upon us will fall the never-ceasing task of keeping that optimum environment for life which is now so freely given.

October 21, 1979

Revisioning Columbus

THE RIGHT REVEREND SIR PAUL REEVES

In the name of God, Creator, redeemer, and giver of life, Amen. It's been hard to follow the bacteria, the elephants, the camels, but I can only do my best, and it's good to be here. And as a guest in this country, I'm continually amazed by the number and the frequency of public holidays you have. Columbus Day is different now. As we know, the fifteenth century was an age of exploration, and the great names were Magellan and Balboa. Certainly, Magellan's exploits excelled those of Columbus. He faced rougher seas, negotiated more treacherous passages, and found his way across a broader ocean. Magellan even commanded a more mutinous crew.

But it is Columbus we remember. We know that after a thirty-three-day journey, he made a landfall in what we now call the Dominican Republic, where under Columbus's governship, fifty thousand native people died. And in his report of that first encounter, Columbus wrote that the "natives were so free with all that they have that no one would believe it who has not seen it. Of anything they possess if it be asked of them, they never say no. On the contrary they invite you to share it and show as much love as if their hearts went with it, and they are content with whatever trifle be given them."

Those are very ominous words. And to the Catholic majesties in Spain, Columbus promised gold, spices, slaves—he said as many as they shall order—rhubarb, and cinnamon. But Columbus was not a savage. He was not like a beachcomber who crosses beaches alone, existing as a stranger in a new society and as a scandal to the old. A beachcomber is confronted with the relativity of his own values and judgments. The beach becomes the place where this new arrival experiments in new ways with wives, children, relations, and property. Columbus had no intention of being a beachcomber. He had no intention of learning from the Indians. And botany was his happy hunting ground. A shrub that smelled like cinnamon, he called cinnamon. A small inedible nut he mistook for the coconut described by Marco Polo. And a root pronounced by the ship's doctor to be the medicinal Chinese rhubarb was really the common garden rhubarb that we forced down the throats of our children.

As Frederick Jackson Turner in his famous 1893 essay on the significance of the frontier in American history said, "The existence of an area of free land, its continuous recession, and the advance of American settlement westward, explains American development." More bluntly, a bumper sticker protesting against gun laws reads, "The West was not won without a gun." True. By the end of the nineteenth century, the indigenous population of what is now Canada and the United States totaled about two hundred and fifty thousand. In pre-European times, it numbered about ten million. "The United States is a Pacific power," wrote Richard Nixon in 1967. "Both our interests and our ideals propel us westward across the Pacific."

The 1971 Academy Award-winning documentary on the My-Lai veterans contained this dialogue: "They cut ears off a guy and stuff like this here without knowing if they were Vietcong or not. Like scalps, you know. Like from Indians." And no wonder that air and ground operations in Vietnam were called Rolling Thunder, Prairie, Sam Houston, Hickory, Daniel Boone, and Crazy Horse, even. Perhaps there is a universal pattern here which in other circumstances would require us to talk about the British in Australia, or the conquistadors in South America. And it's no consolation to say that the violence of white men toward the Indian is more than matched by the violence of white men toward each other.

The facts are that in this march westward, each frontier was won by a series of wars, what the victors call the Indian wars. The movement west has always been a movement of force and conflict. In fact, you could say the disposition of Native Americans has been a defining and enabling experience of this country, defining in the sense that societies are known by their victims. The Indian has been of critical importance for the colonist's understanding of who he is not. So on one side, we're the children of light: the light of the gospel of law, order and progress, freedom and modernization. And on the other side, we are the children of darkness: savages, fiends, special targets, to use the language of Vietnam.

There are two elements here. The first is repression. For the saints of seventeenth-century Massachusetts, going native was really going nature. Increase Mather said, "People are ready to run wild into the woods again and to be as heathenish as ever, if you don't prevent it." From this viewpoint, your body is converted from being an instrument of pleasure into an instrument of domination and aggression. European civilization, in my understanding, defines a person in a very narrow way. The emphasis is on the protection in law of the individual. There is a growing spirit in religion on individual responsibility, and of course there is the endorsement of all the capitalist graces of competition and achievement. Virtue, however you can conceive it, is something which protects you from your environment, rather than binding you to it. Repression.

The second element is the deadly subtlety of the racism which reduces native people to the levels of flora and fauna which, as impediments to this irresistible westward march, have to be removed. The Indian becomes the person on the shore. The person outside the boat. The nonperson living somehow within the settlement culture.

Now what might begin to turn that around is the fact that Vietnam was a break in the historical sequence. Americans and their allies, including people from my country, hurled themselves westward against a human barrier that resisted and defeated them. We lost the war in Vietnam. People should be learning that a workable world mentality means that we have to make peace with those who are different from us. That means the Vietnamese, and it means the Indian. It means all outsiders of this society who remain still to be discovered: to be discovered within their history, their art, their literature, and within their political aspirations. It means getting beyond old images and stereotyping, and it means dealing with the hurt of injustice, the cost of reconciliation, and the search for peace.

As a Maori from New Zealand, who is now involved with indigenous issues at the United Nations, I'm grateful that we were colonized not by the French, or by the Americans, but by the British: the British who at that time were determined to improve on their rather lamentable performance in Australia. But issues in New Zealand and the issues in this country have a common ring to them. That's why we have an Anglican Indigenous Network. That's why indigenous people next month who are Anglicans and who come from New Zealand, from Hawaii, from the United States, and from Canada, will meet near Honolulu in order to help each other. The first item on the agenda will be self-determination and power sharing within the structures of the Church. We shall talk about issues of liturgy. We will discuss what we hope is a loving conversation between traditional spiritualities and the message which came with the missionary who arrived at the same time as the trainer and the soldier. We shall talk about ministry. What does a ministry of native people, for native people, trained by native people, look like? And lastly, we shall talk about the sharing of resources.

But if we want to live at peace with those who differ from us, above all that means understanding ourselves: understanding where our hopes and where our fears come from. Why was there such a compulsion to go west? What were these people running away from?

If I may say so, the real epic of America is the yet-unfinished story of the transformation of the white man.

October 11, 1992

Lessons and Results of Rio

MAURICE STRONG

The Earth Summit in Rio de Janeiro was a challenge, indeed, perhaps the ultimate challenge, to our sense of stewardship. It's stewardship for the planet, yet, a stewardship for the planet that can only be fulfilled in the stewardship we exercise over our own life energies and resources.

What did we really accomplish in Rio? I'm often asked that question these days, and, believe me, I will not give you the long answer to it this morning, because we did a great deal at Rio. The question is: Was it a success? Well, let me remind you that the perspective in which we must view success is perhaps a little longer one than the time that now separates us from the conference.

Henry Kissinger tells a story of his first meeting with chairman Mao. The two were awkwardly trying to break the ice, and they touched on the subject of revolutions. Kissinger said to Mao that although ideologically he did not agree with the Chinese revolution, he did agree that it had accomplished certain things for China. Kissinger says, "I asked the Chairman, just to keep the conversation going, 'What do you think, Mr. Chariman, were the real effects of the French Revolution?'" And he reports that Chairman Mao looked at him benignly and said, "Well, Mr. Kissinger, it's a little early to tell."

Well, it is certainly a little too early to tell what will be the ultimate results of Rio. As a political event, however, it was a historic one. In terms of engagement, we engaged more people, more constituencies, more organizations, more sectors of society in the two and a half years of preparations for the conference, and at the conference iself, than had ever participated in any world event. We also engaged the attention of the media, more than double the media than have ever been accredited to any world gathering. So the people of the world, through the media, were intimately involved in the experience as well.

What did we do? Well, we had more leaders than have ever gathered together. It was fitting that those leaders were gathered to make decisions that will literally effect the future of life on our planet.

What did they agree on? Quite a lot. Attention has been concentrated on what they did not agree on, and of course there were a number of things upon which they did not agree. What is remarkable, however, is that the leaders of 180 nations of the world could agree on a set of principles, the Declaration of Rio, and the most comprehensive and far-ranging program of action ever agreed to by a world community, Agenda 21, the agenda for the twenty-first century. Not perfect, of course; not fully complete, of course; but, if we follow and implement that agenda, we will be on the pathway to that more secure and sustainable future for which the Earth Summit was convened.

The results of the conference, the Declaration, Agenda 21, the conventions that were agreed and signed by over 150 nations there, do in fact provide the basic foundations for the change of course that we must make. Change will occur. Change is occurring. The only real question is, will that change be a willed and skillfully managed change on the part of the human community, or will it be forced on us by nature's revenge for our lack of stewardship?

Only willed change will assure a sustainable and secure future. And that change depends on us, in particular on the people who live in the industrialized countries.

The change relies more particularly on those of this great country which decided on an important change of course during this past week. This change presents a new opportunity for a re-establishment of leadership of this great nation, the United States, as we move into the twenty-first century. We, we who call ourselves Christians, we who are products of the Judeo-Christian tradition, are the primary source today of the threats that confront our planet and the future of life on it. We have lost our innocence because what we may have been doing in the past inadvertently, we are now doing knowingly. Surely that sin must impose itself on our conscience.

The Rio Declaration sets out twenty-seven basic principles that must drive our change of course. Let me cite just a few of them and what they mean, in my view, to Christians. The first principle is that human beings are at the center of concerns for sustainable development. They are entitled to a healthy and productive life in harmony with nature, not dominion over nature with a sense of unrestrained exploitation of nature.

We must move beyond the concept of dominion articulated by the moderator of the Church of Scotland in 1930 when he said, "This world exists for our sake and not for its own." A lot of sincere Christians did in fact hold that view. Fortunately, it has been largely put aside by the Christian community of today; however, the habits and the practices to which it gave rise unhappily continue to entrench themselves in our society and in our personal lives.

We must see our relationship with Earth in terms of stewardship and redemption. The affinity between Christ and nature is clear from many passages of the Bible, as in Matthew's account of the crucifixion when he says that the Earth itself demonstrated its agony at the crucifixion of Christ. There was darkness all over the land, the Earth shook, rocks were split, the curtain of the temple was split in two, and tombs were shaken open. In Chapters 38 and 39 of the book of Job, the relationship between God, the Creator of humankind and nature are invoked when God says, "Where were you when I laid the foundations of the Earth? . . . When the morning stars sang together and all the sons of God shouted for joy." The Earth and the Christian tradition are deeply and inextricably linked, far more than the oft-quoted and discarded concept of an exploited dominion over the Earth. Today most Christians realize that we have a special responsibility not to exploit nature but to exercise stewardship over it. Our lifestyles and developmental modes are still not in harmony with nature.

Principle three of the declaration describes the right to development and makes it clear that we have an obligation not only to our present generation but to future generations on this planet. This requires stewardship again and responsibility to those who will succeed us. The obligation to develop sustainably so that, in the words of the Bruntland Commission, their future right to meet their needs will not be compromised by what we do in meeting ours.

The fifth principle, "All states and people shall cooperate in the essential task of eradicating poverty," is an indispensable requirement for sustainable development. This is not just an idle statement, but one negotiated and accepted by the nations of all the world. We must recognize poverty not just as great moral crime but, as an unsustainable condition. Blessed are the poor in spirit. Christ to the rich man said, "Sell all you have and give it to the poor." Poverty is the denial of a moral basis for our civilization as well as a threat to our environmental future. Yet in our Christian societies, disparities between rich and poor are deepening. The same is true internationally. There is a great challenge that has come out of the Earth Summit, a challenge to make the eradication of poverty a central objective of the world community in the twenty-first century. We will either have, I predict, a new rich/poor partnership as reflected in Agenda 21, or we will slide into a rich/poor war.

Principle number seven describes the special responsibility of industrialized societies like ours. We have a command of technology. We have a disproportionate share of the world's financial resources. We are called upon to exercise the responsibility, the stewardship which that requires for those who are disadvantaged in our own society and those who share in other countries the fate of our planet with us.

Principle number eight calls on us to reduce and eliminate the unsustainable patterns of production and consumption in which we Christians indulge to the ultimate degree. It is, in fact, our indulgence that has produced the new generation of risks to our planet. Yes, perhaps we did it innocently, but as I mentioned earlier, we have lost our innocence. Can we continue to do this? These patterns of consumption and production are clearly not sustainable for us and are not helpful to the rest of the world. We must again lead the way to change, not back to a primitive, self-sacrificing, hair-shirt type of life, but to lives of sophisticated modesty. Lives which are made possible now by technology. The same technology that has helped create the problem can be invoked as an ally in reshaping our patterns of production and consumption.

Principle ten is the whole principle of citizen participation, the need for people's participation. This was the key to Rio, it was the key to bringing the world leaders to Rio, it was the key to the pressure that was on those leaders to make the agreements they made at Rio, and it will also be the key to their implementation. I was privileged to address these world leaders on a number of occasions, and at the end, I said that I appreciated them and was grateful and hopeful for them for the agreements that they had reached. I was afraid, though, that much of it represented agreement without commitment. It will be the people who must insure that those agreements are accompanied by the commitment required to make them effective. And related to that, the whole question of not using trade measures to unilaterally impose our values and our priorities on others. On insuring that those who may be affected by our actions, internally and across national borders, have access to all the information they need on initiatives which may indeed affect that. The whole principle of compensation referred to in principle thirteen stems from the fact that when we do damage people, it's not just interpersonally, it's from nation to nation. Every moment that goes by, our countries—United States, my own country Canada, and the other industrialized nations of the world—are inflicting damage to the health, to the economies, and to the resource space of people all over the world. We are doing it now, we are continuing to do it. The principle calls us to accountability and indeed, culpability—to make compensation for doing that. These are tough things.

I have to say that the principles were very hard to negotiate. In many cases the word *shall* was weakened to *should*. The fundamental principle is still quite clear in each case, however. Also calling in other principles, of the twenty-seven, for the special recognition for the special role of participation and support of which our civilization has robbed them. These principles, and the programs of Agenda 21 which give effect to them, provide the basis for the shifting direction we need to take to insure that our Earth does indeed remain a secure and hospitable home for present and future generations. They are fully consistent with Christian principles, and through them we could literally save the Earth. We could harp on how much we might improve the wording of these principles, but we must not wait to give effect to them in our own lives, and the finger is pointed at us, who call ourselves Christians, to take the lead because it is consistent with everything we say we stand for.

Last Tuesday, an event of historic importance took place in this country: the election of a new president and vice president. Perhaps it was something even more than that. A new generation of leaders is coming into play in the United States and the world, one which will lead us into the twenty-first century. I am convinced by all the evidence that I have seen in my more than two decades of involvement in these issues, and particularly in my preparations for the Earth Summit in Rio, that what we do or fail to do in the remainder of this century will determine, perhaps decisively, the future course of life on our planet. So it is in no narrow partisan sense that I say that we look to this new leadership team with special hope, with great expectations.

Rarely have we had the opportunity to access the deep incisive values which will influence this administration more than we have through Vice President-elect Al Gore's book, *Earth in the Balance: Ecology and the Human Spirit*. I recommend that all of you read it whether you agree with all of his observations, his analysis, and his prescriptions or not. They will be important to the future of this country, important if you understand them. It is deeply encouraging for me to know that these are the views and the values that will be at the very heart of the new administration. We do not know for certain what President-elect Clinton thinks about them, but we can assume that he thinks highly of them or he would not have chosen Al Gore as his running mate. I like to think it is one of the reasons that he chose Al Gore as his running mate.

Consider finally just a few of the things that Al Gore, a committed Christian, says in his book. These are, in my view, encouraging, indeed revolutionary. He says, "There is little doubt that the way we currently relate to the environment is widely inappropriate. In order to change, we have to address the fundamental questions about our own purpose in life . . . [and about] an appropriate technology to respond to these challenges to the Earth. These questions are not for the mind or the body, but for the spirit." Then when he acknowledges his own tradition, he says the purpose of life, his life, is to glorify God.

There is a shared conviction, he says, within the Judeo-Christian tradition that believers are expected to do justice, love mercy, and walk humbly with our God. But how, he asks, can one walk humbly with nature's God while wreaking havoc on nature? Then he points out how the idea of social justice is inextricably linked to the scriptures and with ecology. In passage after passage, environmental degradation and social injustice go hand in hand. In today's world the links between social injustice and environmental degradation can be seen everywhere: in the placement of disproportionate levels of lead and toxic waste in poor neighborhoods, the devastation of indigenous people and the extinction of their cultures when the rainforests are destroyed, the corruption of many government officials by people who seek to profit from unsustainable exploitation of resources. Finally he says, "It is my view that the underlying moral schism that contributed to these extreme manifestations of evil has also conditioned our civilization to insulate its conscience from any responsibility for the collective endeavors that visibly link millions of small, silent, banal acts and omissions together in a pattern of terrible cause and effect." Today we enthusiastically participate in what is, in essence, a massive and unprecedented experiment with the natural system of the global environment with little regard for its moral consequences. We tolerate and collectively perpetrate all that is now going on. Future generations will wonder how we can go along with our daily routines in silent complicity with the collective destruction of the Earth. Will we, like the unfaithful servant, claim that we did not notice these things because we were morally asleep? Is that what we will feign? Or will we try to explain that we were not so much asleep as living in a walking trance, a strange Cartesian spell, under whose influence we felt no connection between our routine banal acts and the moral consequences of what we did as long as we were far away and at the other end of the massive machine of civilization? What, Gore asks, would future generations say in response to such a pitiful plea?

Now that this kind of analysis and this kind of thinking—about the connection between the dilemma which world leaders confronted at Rio and the personal spiritual value systems that motivate us in our lives and careers—has been brought into the very center of power in this great country at a fateful time in the history of the Earth, and at a time when U.S. leadership has never been more indispensable to the future of the planet. Surely that is prophetic, surely that is hopeful, surely that imposes on the Clinton–Gore team, and all of us, whatever our political partnership, a need to commit ourselves to the larger issues that unite us and move beyond the diviseness of economic trade wars and participant election campaigns. I have to say that the Earth Summit has no better champion than Al Gore. From its inception he was one of our best supporters, and now we look to him and the team around him and the people who will be supporting him, to take the lead in insuring that the hopes and expectations engendered in the Earth Summit will in fact be realized. But our leaders cannot do it alone. The Earth Summit was a result of the exercise of people's power on a massive scale.

Unprecedented people's input and interest and awareness made it possible. This must continue. It's why I am involved with many others in the creation of an Earth Council as a complement, supplement, and support for the official commisison on sustainable development that will hopefully be set up by the United Nations. To ensure that the continuous focus by an informed, concerned, and active public on the issues of Rio and on the need to hold leaders accountable for what they do or fail to do in response to those agreements. Today, Christians surely are challenged as never before to live up to the basic tenants of their faith. Why? Because we are at the center. Highest expectations rest on our shoulders. As Paul said in his Epistle to the Romans, "We knew that the whole of Creation had been groaning in travail together until now, not only Creation, but ourselves." The theme we chose for the Summit, "In our hands," is very real. The future of our planet, the change of course set for our planet is literally in our hands. In the hands of each of us individually as well as collectively.

November 8, 1992

St. Francis Day

CARL SAGAN

In his *Life of St. Francis*, St. Bonaventure wrote, "When he bethought himself of the first beginning of all things, he [that is, St. Francis] was filled with a yet more overflowing charity and would call the dumb animals howsoever small by the names of brother and sister for as much as he recognized in them the same origin as in himself." The idea that all the beings of the natural world have a common origin in a way prefigured by St. Francis was brought to scientific fruition just a little more than a hundred years ago by Charles Darwin, who, but for a bit of happenstance, would probably have lived out his days as a Church of England parson in a quiet country town in England.

Given his religious background, it seems to me that Charles Darwin ought also to be one of the saints of the Episcopal Church. He did not intend to upset the apple cart, but he had so deep a commitment to truth that what he saw in his round-the-world voyage on the ship *Beagle*, forced him to conclude that species are not immutable, that organisms have evolved one from another, and that the planet must be far older than the conventional belief of his day could conceive. This was the only way to explain the immense vistas of time needed for such evolution.

Darwin's great insights have been fully and profoundly confirmed in our own time, among other ways by the new science of molecular biology. Life on Earth began some four billion years ago from very simple and humble beginnings, and has produced the gorgeous diversity that we see around us today. The evolutionary process has made the Earth brim over with life. There are beings that walk, jump, hop, fly, glide, flute, slither, burrow, stride on the water's surface, canter, waddle, brachiate, swim, tumble and patiently wait. Damsel flies molt, deciduous trees bud, great cats stalk, antelopes take fright, birds chatter, nematodes worry a grain of humus, perfect insect imitations of leaves and twigs rest incognito on a branch. Earth worms entwine themselves in passionate bisexual embrace. Algae and fungi are comfortable roommates in the lichen partnership. Great whales sing their plaintive songs as they traverse the world ocean. Willows suck moisture from unseen underground aquifers and a universe of microbes swarms in every thimbleful of muck. There is hardly a clod of soil, a drop of water, a breath of air, that is not teeming with life. And I might add, so far as we know, this is not true of all the worlds in our solar system, only of the Earth.

Life fills every nook and cranny of our planet's surface. There are bacteria in the upper air, jumping spiders at the tops of the highest mountains, sulphur-metabolizing worms in the deep ocean trenches, and heat-loving microbes kilometers below the surface of the land. Almost all these beings are in intimate contact. They eat and drink one another, breathe each other's waste gases, inhabit one another's bodies, disguise themselves to look like one another, construct intricate networks of mutual cooperation, and gratuitously fiddle with each other's genetic instructions. They have generated a web of mutual dependence and interaction that embraces the planet.

We are part of that web. We are dependent upon it. And yet we are profoundly ignorant about the connections. So in the great tapestry of life, if we pull out one thread, we do not always know whether the harm done is just to that thread or whether in consequence we will unravel much of the tapestry. We must be very careful with regard to what fate we hold in store for the other beasts and vegetables who inhabit this planet with us. Part of the concern for the global environment is a concern for ourselves directly, and part is a concern for ourselves indirectly because of our deep connection with other even more vulnerable organisms, and third, a part is because we recognize that these beings have as profound and extended an evolutionary history as we and as much a right to live as we.

There is another, profound reason why we should treasure these other beings: because we can understand ourselves better by understanding them. Our nearest biological relatives are the chimpanzees. We share 99.6 per cent of our active genes with them. The only hereditary difference between us and chimps are .4 per cent of the genetic material. You might say that that .4 per cent must be responsible for very great differences, but you also might say that the differences are not as great as we pretend. And much of human society—not how we pretend we act but how we really act—is in many respects, in my view, indistinguishable from everyday life among the chimps.

One of the great human achievements has been to explore the other worlds in the solar system. We have sent spacecrafts to the farthest reaches of our solar system, and four of them are in the process of leaving the solar system, bound to wander forever in the great dark between the stars. When one of them, Voyager One, finished its planetary mission, we were able to turn it around so that it could photograph some of the worlds that it had passed close by but from a now-immense distance.

One picture that I very much wanted to take—which we finally were able to take—was a picture of the Earth from the outskirts of the solar system. And there it was, a single pixel, or a single picture element, a pale blue dot. No continents, no national boundaries, no beings, no humans, just a dot. That's us. That's where we live. That's where everyone we know, everyone we love, everyone we ever heard of, every human being who ever lived has lived: on that pale blue dot. Every hopeful child, every couple in love, every prince and pauper, every revered religious leader, every corrupt politician, every scientist, every humble person living out his or her days—all of us—every one of us and all the other beings, live on that pale blue dot.

To me it underscores our responsibility, because you look at that dot and you think how fragile and vulnerable it is. Our central responsibility is to cherish and care for the environment on the only home we have ever known and the only home for all those other beings with whom we are so profoundly connected.

October 3, 1993

* III *
NATURE, GOD, AND US

Heaven Sent Home

THE REV. MINKA SHURA SPRAGUE

*W*e seek a rest, a space of quiet
we yearn for the mystery that lives within us
we pray for the source that calls all things to communion

we turn
we turn to remember
   the mystery that lies within us

we turn
we turn to remember
   our selves, who God is

we turn
we turn to remember
   bound in the strong name of the Trinity, the design

     "As you leave Eden behind you, remember your home
     For as you remember back into your own being
     You will not be alone; the first to greet you
     Will be those children playing by the burn
     The otters will swim up to you in the bay
     The wild deer on the moor will run beside you.
     Recollect more deeply, and the birds will come,
     Fish rise to meet you in their silver shoals
     And darker, stranger, more mysterious lives
     Will throng about you at the source
     Where the tree's deepest roots drink from the abyss."

we turn
our words, our wonder
    winding their way around
    recalling older words to speak design
    remembering source
        God from God, Light from Light
        the waters, separated from waters
    landing, our words, on the light and on the air

        "Earth sends a mother's love after her exiled [child]
         Entrusting her message to the light and the air
         The wind and waves that carry your ship, the rain that falls
         The birds that call to you, and all the shoals
         That swim in the natal waters of her ocean."

suddenly, beyond guilt, forgiveness known
our turning, our wonder
    safe in the liturgy's arm
    have the grasslands prayed for us these 20 million years?

    bound by the Trinity, safe in the liturgy's arms
    suddenly, we glimpse
        "darker, stranger, more mysterious lives"
         our source, thronging about us, one source
         does slow stone heartbeat whisper love and care for us?

    for us, for us
    turning
        "with farther to travel from our simplicity
         from the archaic moss, fish and lily parts. . ."

    for us, for us
    turning
        "in exile traveling our long way"

    for us?

    our words wind around, landing on light and air
    Earth's mother's love for her exiled child
    for us, for us

to ask after us
safe in the liturgy's arms
in communion, one source
the rain is here to wash our face

the heavens, more mysterious lives
the ocean's shoals, animals we have called "pets"
archaic moss, fish and lily parts
they wonder about us
will they remember, children of the sixth day
image of God, dust of our dust
    will they remember
    "the ultimate memory"?

    will they remember
    "of all created things the source is one"?

    will they, image and dust, come home?
    to memory, to love
    "to sleep at the tree's root, where the night is spun
     into the stuff of worlds"?

    will they remember to listen?
    ".. to listen to the winds
     the tides, and the night's harmonies and know
     All that they knew before they began to forget
     Before they became estranged from their own being"?

our words, Trinity-bound in communion
land on light and air, breath on Creation's breath herself
    breath of God to image of God
    Holy Spirit inhalation
    to ask

    will my children slide into their sixth day
    and find it Heaven?

    find Creation, home? accept Creation's love?
    take Creation's prayer, forgiveness known?

the light, the air, slow-heartbeat stone
toss our words of wonder in communion
    until we remember
    we want to remember
      the light separated from the darkness
      waters from soil, vegetation up-springing
      a first, a second, a third day

    until we remember
    we want to remember
      lights to separate day from night
      for signs and seasons, days and years
      a greater light given dominion of it all
      a fourth day

    breath of God to image of God
on light and air, winding their way
    until we remember we want to remember
      our place at the close of day six
      waters bringing forth swimming ones
      air bringing forth flying ones
      Earth bringing forth
      walking ones, creeping ones, wild ones
      and we, one image, two genders
      image of God, dust of this Earth
      brought forth from God and Earth
      God and Creation in concert, one source
      it is last, we remember
      our place

we remember we want to remember
Creation of Earth, image of God
    to hear
    "Earth sends a mother's love after her exiled child"

    to meet
    "darker, stranger, more mysterious lives"

to be
dust we are, image of God, two genders true

to come home
at the close of the sixth day

to turn, Trinity-bound
safe in the liturgy's arms

accepting forgiveness
cleaning our waste
learning how little enough can be
beholding the abundance of communion
reminding our selves

all is connected, everything matters
Creation coheres, nothing is lost
love is never, never lost
never

safe in the liturgy's arms
Trinity-bound, making communion
turning, turning
to light and air, dancing our words

to remember oh yes, we want to remember
our place
the design, Heaven sent home
that God saw all that God had made
and behold, it was very good
a sixth day

very good

very good
Heaven sent home

[This sermon / prose poem incorporates quotes from #8, "Nature", *Special Themes Gates of Prayer, The New Union Prayerbook*, Central Conference of American Rabbis, Jewish Year 5735, New York, 1975.]

"Where Were You When I Created Leviathan?"

THE REV. CARLA BERKEDAL

Job 38:1-12; 18, 22-31, 33
Romans 8:18-25
Mark 4:26-34

If we think back on our lives, we can often see how seemingly small things were, in retrospect, very important. Though we did not know it at the time, by a certain thing happening at just a certain time our life was changed. Missing that "something" by a day or even a few hours would have meant a very different life. More often than not the track on which we were heading was interrupted and our course changed. God interrupted.

Roger Tory Peterson, author of *Field Guide to the Birds*, the birder's Bible, describes the experience that changed his life and set him on the course he was to follow. He called it a trigger. One Saturday he was taking a walk with a friend and came upon a flicker in an oak tree ("or maybe it was a maple"). Thinking the bird was dead, he poked at it, gingerly, the way you touch something you think is dead; but the bird was just asleep, probably resting from migration. When he touched it, its eyes flew open and it flew away. "This inert bunch of feathers suddenly sprang to life." What struck him was the contrast between what he thought was dead but in actuality was very much alive. "Almost like resurrection. . . . Ever since then birds seemed to me the most vivid expression of life."

Three years ago, the popular children's folksinger Raffi took time off to think about where his music should go next. For him, a point was driven home when he learned about how beluga whales are now an endangered species in the St. Lawrence River and that their bodies are so riddled with toxins that when they die, their bodies are classified as toxic waste. Raffi now calls himself a "radical Earth advocate" and is committed to creating music which inspires people to care for the Earth.

Finally, Richard Austin, a Presbyterian minister in southwest Virginia recounts the call to environmental ministry he experienced in 1972: "My parishioners were resisting the ravages of strip mining. . . . I emerged from that struggle convinced that God was calling me to articulate relationships between biblical faith and environmental responsibility."

Wherever I go I hear so many similar stories, from very ordinary people—like the woman who returned to the New Jersey beach of her childhood and found it closed because of medical waste. She left the shore a different woman. These are stories about change. A "wake-up call," as a friend of mine describes her experience of washing oiled birds after an oil spill. That was what woke me up as well. This waking is a deepened awareness of what is, a sudden seeing of an extraordinary experience of the ordinary realized as the extraordinary it is—a bird thought dead which is alive, a whale whose dead body will not nourish, but rather will poison the Earth!

In these moments we are touched by the beauty, fragility, and holiness of the Earth, and we find ourselves summoned to a work that will not wait. Something has been happening in people and more so in recent years than perhaps ever. While planet Earth faces the greatest challenges it has ever known, something is happening in *people* and in our culture.

We are none too early in being roused by our wake-up calls. Each year the Earth loses seventy-six billion tons of topsoil. Between 1550 and 1950, fifteen species per year became extinct. By the year 2000, it is estimated, one hundred species per day will become extinct. Lester Brown, in *State of the Earth,* encapsulates the status of planet Earth, and the responsibility of our generation very well: "Ours is the first generation faced with decisions that will determine whether the Earth our children inherit is habitable."

Can you comprehend this? *Can anyone?* People may disagree as to which environmental problems are most pressing, what timelines are the most accurate—climatologists and scientists rarely concur—but few experts disagree that the coming ten years are critical for turning around the course on which modern humans have been traveling. For, of course, we humans are the endangered species. The task we face is to preserve the world in some wholeness for the generations yet unborn.

"Where were you when I laid the Earth's foundations?" For centuries, the story of Job has humbled and comforted the seeking heart. His story has a message, I believe, for our generation. A message of challenge, of hope, and of perspective—a way to see "aright." Job, faithful servant of the Lord, is tested by terrible misfortunes, assailed by so many losses. Poor Job is comforted by well-meaning but unhelpful friends ("Don't just do something; stand there!"). At last Job is encountered by the Holy One; the One who calls forth life responds from the whirlwind. Then Job the questioner is himself questioned. "Where were you when I laid the foundations of the world?"

The key word throughout is *understanding.* Do *you* understand? Can you create? The questions are exquisitely detailed. Can you tell the mother doe when her time for delivery is nigh (Job's wife would have been very pleased if Job could have done just that!). God is not just showing off here, he is also showing Job who he is, and the context in which, alone, his life has meaning and his suffering has its place.

When the voice from the whirlwind surrounds him, Job realizes how infinitely small he is in the vast cosmos. Human beings are small; they are small *before God.* Job begins to know his place. He feels small but not insignificant. It is the difference between the insignificance we feel at the foot of a city skyscraper, and the tininess we feel at the foot of Mt. Rainier. Our foot at the foot of Mt. Rainier, we feel connected to God, we know our place, we know we belong.

And why? Because Creation itself is an avenue of communion between Creator and creature. God reveals Godself here, within the majesty, and sometimes the terror, of the Creation. God has given human beings wisdom—not the wisdom to fully penetrate the mysteries of nature, but God has endowed us with the unique and precious gift of *seeing* the Creator *in the world the Creator has made.*

God touched Job in his suffering. God did not answer all of Job's questions. Actually, God did not answer *any* of his questions, but after his encounter with God, the autumn leaf feathering down from the tree, the sound of a stream at dawn, would always speak to Job of God. The world had become for him as for Gerard Manley Hopkins, "charged with the glory of God."

It is fascinating to note when Job finally listens: his questioning is silenced at the very moment when God's Creation has become the answer to the question of Job's own existence. Put eloquently by the Jewish scholar, Margaret Susman, "This is not accomplished by Job's understanding of the order of Creation and the role his own suffering plays in it. On the contrary, he does not understand, and that is his answer. He does not want to understand. There is nothing for him to understand; in humility he has accepted his own place in God's Creation and in doing so, he has said yes to his own suffering."

And so, I believe, God is asking questions of this generation. God's questions are turned to us. And the questions come to us not as accusations but as judgment. They come as wisdom and comfort and hope.

We Christians take for granted the idea of God as Creator. Every Sunday we say the creed, "I believe in God the Father Almighty, Creator of Heaven and Earth." Yet we rarely make the connection that the God to whom we pray is also the God of all that has life. The Word whom we worship as the Christ was also the Word who breathed all life into being on the morning of the first day. We forget that the Christ who is our Lord is also the Lord of all Creation.

You see, what Job learned, finally, was to accept the terms of Creation, not with defiance, but with joy and gratitude. Wendell Berry, a poet and the closest to the modern-day incarnation of Job that I know, says that what we need *to do is to learn to experience our dependence on other living things,* and ultimately, I would add, upon God, with gratitude. "For we are living from mystery, from creatures we did not make and powers we cannot comprehend."

When we have been summoned, when some powerful experience wakes us up and opens us to the truth that we are living from mystery, then the Church has a tremendous perspective which, I deeply believe, can keep us on track. "I believe in God, Creator of Heaven and Earth." In other words, God, we believe, is revealed first of all in the things of this world, that is to say, in the Creation itself. Christians are not Platonists! Unlike Platonism, Christianity does not view this world as just a shadow, pointing away from itself, not of the real world elsewhere. Rather, Christians hold a sacramental view of the world. *There are no ordinary things.*

John Keble, Anglican divine, writing on the Desert Fathers said of their view of life, "Everything is capable of becoming a means of grace. . . . The whole world, to them, was full of sacraments." So, the water which we use at baptism, the bread and wine we bring to the eucharistic table are not accidental items, they represent, in the deepest sense, a world which to the person of faith is in every part, a gift of God's love for us.

Again, the modern Job, Wendell Berry, expresses the Christian understanding of sacrament so powerfully to me: "I do not mean to suggest we can live harmlessly or strictly at our own expense; we depend upon other creatures and survive by their deaths. To live, we must daily break the body and shed the blood of Creation." The point is, he continues, "When we do this knowingly, lovingly, skillfully, reverently, it is a sacrament. When we do it ignorantly, greedily, clumsily, destructively, it is a desecration. . . . In such desecration we condemn ourselves to spiritual and moral loneliness and others to want."

And so, in a few moments, we will break bread and drink wine. We will take the common, everyday things of our life and give thanks. We will eat consciously, gratefully.

We will also be invited by Bishop Warner to renew our baptismal vows. In recalling our beginnings in the faith, we will also be reminded of the beginning of the world. God created the world and blessed it and called it good and gave to human beings and other creatures the Earth as food and life and as the means of communion with him. As the bishop will stand before the baptismal font, as if facing the great waters on the day of Creation, he will give thanks for the waters of life and of salvation and in so doing he will acknowledge the true nature of things—we receive life from God, we depend every moment upon God's gift of life. So as we renew our baptismal vows we turn from death to choose life, to living consciously, gratefully, and therefore with joy and wonder in all of God's work.

We live in a challenging generation, staggeringly so. If one believes even the more moderate statistics and predictions, this is a frightening time to be alive. If by God's grace, we are interrupted and awakened to the travail of the Earth, we need to learn to trust these experiences, be faithful to these interruptions. Our generation has the spiritual calling to live in a profoundly sacramental way. If our sin is to have denied our reliance on God for the gift of life, our restoration to right relationship with God is to acknowledge our dependence on God and on God's gift of life, which we know only on this Earth.

Like Job, we are definitely not patient, nor do we understand why things are the way they are. In many cases, we see only dimly in which direction the solutions lie. But I believe the Gospel. I also believe that the future does not depend upon human wisdom to change our course alone. We can say "yes" to the challenges of our times because we trust in the God who can make a forest out of a few seeds.

Water, mustard seeds, bread and wine—the gifts of God for the people of God. God will take our offerings of love and work and hope, and though we know not how, God will transform our offerings into life. What we do know is that long ago history was interrupted and a child was born in Bethlehem, a seemingly small and insignificant event. Yet it was not. We know that that child born in Bethlehem calls us and is faithful to that call. Each of us, molded and shaped by what we have suffered, like God's servant Job, in our own unique way will do the work that needs to be done.

In the name of the One without whom all our striving would be losing, Amen.

February 26, 1992

St. Francis and Lady Poverty

DEAN JAMES PARKS MORTON

Not long ago in Rio de Janeiro, 180 nations of the world came together under the auspices of the United Nations to legislate Mother Earth, to ask hard questions and to make tough decisions about a green, vibrant, living, sustaining planet—about poverty and justice and jobs and the southern hemisphere. This is the first St. Francis Day after we have seen that greenness and Somalia go together. Many people will say that Rio did not produce much, and certainly we would all say Rio did not produce as much as it might have. But everyone now speaks of the "world after Rio." Rio was a kind of global moment of truth. And there is no going back. Rio made all of us global citizens, not just New Yorkers or Americans. And therefore on November 3 when we go to the polls, we must be responsible about both greenness and poverty.

Dear friends, dear sisters, dear brothers, the really remarkable thing about today in the light of Rio is that six hundred years ago St. Francesco, the little brother from Assisi, was really the first modern citizen. St. Francis was really the first planetary citizen who brought together in his own flesh both the embracing of poverty and the love of the Earth. So St. Francis is really our most contemporary role model for the twenty-first century. I want to say only four things about St. Francis this morning that I hope can bind him to us and to our responsibility of being loving and faithful global twenty-first-century citizens, citizens who can somehow escape the dual trap between sentimentality about the Earth and, on the other hand, grim doomsday humorlessness. We've got to escape these two.

I am going to talk about four aspects of St. Francis: about his poverty, about his understanding of communion, about his experience with the cross, and about his experience with joy.

First, poverty. For St. Francis, poverty is not grim. Poverty is a gift. Poverty is beautiful. He speaks of "lady poverty." Poverty is the key to everything for St. Francis. The key is being free of objects. Being open to receive and to give because for Francis it is all God's Creation of which we are all stewards, all caretakers, all lovers, but not owners. As Chief Seattle said, how can you own the air, how can you own the sun, how can you own the trees, how can you own the Earth? Possessions are a delusion. Poverty is a wonderful open dance of exchanging gifts given by God. Poverty makes thanksgiving, gratitude, and hubris possible. Poverty allows us to be the richest people on Earth because we share the sun's warmth and beauty and all of the Earth's bounty. Poverty is that wonderful understanding of who we really are. We are wonderful stardust, and we will return to stardust: this is what makes it possible for St. Francis to speak of Brother Sun and Sister Fire and Mother Earth and Sister Death. In poverty, all are gifts to share.

The second aspect is communion. Communion is the state of coming together in union. It proceeds directly from the openness of poverty; it is poverty in action. We do not possess; we do not own. We share. My bread is your bread because it is God's bread. My body is your body because it is God's body. My Earth is your Earth because it is God's Earth. The Earth is also God's body, Corpus Christi.

Ecology and *communion* are similar words because both describe the indwelling, the coinherence of parts in the whole. For Francis, the wolf was his brother, the forest was his sister, and the Earth was his mother. Francis was in communication with nature and was in communion with nature. Therefore, he was in communion and in communication with animals. Men and women the world over have always experienced this communion, and they have always spoken with other species. St. Francis spoke with the birds and with the wolves. St. Sergis and St. Seraphim in Russia in the forest spoke with the animals. For them, the eagle was an angel, the true messenger of God's word.

Francis was in communion with the Earth all of his life. Communion means crossing all barriers, drinking the bitter with the sweet. There is no sentimentality in communion. Jesus said, "Shall this cup be taken away?"

No, he drank it to the dregs, and he shares it with us. Drink this all of you. The Earth is God's body and God's blood is the Earth's suffering, and we are all asked to eat and to drink of the gift of both. Communion is the gift of life itself, and it is God's gift to all of us.

The third thing about Francis is the cross. Communion, drinking to the dregs, real sharing, real poverty, real openness, genuine coinherence, true in-dwelling: all of these lead to pain, death, the most difficult gifts of all. Yet Francis knelt in the tiny ancient ruined chapel of Saint Damiano before the great crucifix with its wonderful open eyes, the live Christ.

Three times in Francis's life, the cross spoke to him, and Jesus said, "Build my Church." The first time, Francis was a young man, and when the cross spoke to him, Francis thought very literally. He became a stone mason, and he retored St. Damiano. He then organized an order of friars to rebuild other churches. Years later, the cross spoke a second time to Francis and again Jesus said, "Build my Church." Now, St. Francis knew that this meant much more than rebuilding stone churches. He knew that the meaning involved people thoughout the world. He knew that the meaning was political, and it had to do with war and peace and with Christians and Muslims and Jews.

So St. Francis journeyed to Rome to meet with the Pope, and then he journeyed to Egypt to meet with the Sultan, and then he journeyed to Jerusalem to be in the city that is the mother of the three great religions of Abraham. St. Francis was a global man. This humble friar spoke to the highest courts of political power.

Then at the very end of his life, St. Francis again knelt before the living cross at Saint Damiano, and Jesus again, for the third time said, "Build my Church." This time the cross literally left the wall and embraced Francis so that the nail holes in Jesus' hand touched Francis' hand, and the nail holes in Jesus' feet touched Francis' feet, and the gash in Jesus' side touched Francis' heart, and Francis came into full communion with Jesus on the cross.

What was the meaning of these stigmata for Francis? It was pure bliss! This aspect of pure joy is the fourth point of St. Francis' life that is important for us. It's the final gift of life that transcends pleasure and happiness, transcends suffering and pain, even death. Joy, this simple word, joy is the heart of God. Joy is Heaven on Earth. Joy is ecstasy, joy is bliss now, not in the years ahead. Joy binds together poverty and communion and the cross in a kind of sunburst of glory. In that moment in St. Damiano near the end of Francis' life, when he was old and could hardly walk and was in great physical pain, he experienced the peace and the joy that passed all understanding, and what did he do?

He was carried back to his deathbed, and on his deathbed he wrote "The Canticle of the Sun," the great poem that must become the theme song of our post-Rio world and of our whole life in the twenty-first century as men and women of faith and of responsibility.

Our individual life and our global life come together in this ground swell of joy. Joy is the fruit of poverty and openness. Joy is the gift of communion. Joy, like the four directions of the cross, transcends all boundaries of North, South, East, West, Heaven, and Hell. Therefore my brothers and sisters, I invite you to say with me the hymn of ecology which joins greenness and poverty, environment and joy, which joins greenness with Heaven and with Harlem, the first verse of St. Francis' hymn, the hymn of the twenty-first century:

> All praise be yours through Brother Sun
> All praise be yours through Sister Moon
> By Mother Earth my Lord be praised
> By Brother Mountain, Sister Sea, through Brother Wind and Brother
>   Air through Sister Water, Brother Fire.
> The star above give thanks to thee
> All praise to those who live in peace.

St. Francis Day, October 4, 1992

Nature's Faithfulness and Ours

BROTHER DAVID STEINDL-RAST

In Jesus we see what we are meant to be, but we must become it as a community. To be human, to be fully human, means a communal reality, and Jesus is the pioneer of this common reality. The new Adam, the new, full, true human being is inseparable from the kingdom of God, from the peaceable kingdom, from the Earth household. As Gary Snyder says, "From the Earth as the household of God, which the Earth is, except for us humans." Therefore we pray. In all three readings this Sunday, we emphasize the need for prayer and the power of prayer. Therefore we pray for a newer kingdom come, for the community of the son of man come for the fully human community come, for the true human come in community. Every time we pray, "kingdom come," we pray for the coming of the true human in community and in community with the whole Earth. Therefore we pray, "It will be done on Earth as it is done in Heaven."

Heaven is where God's will is already being done. This includes nature. In all of nature, God's will is already done. And Earth is where our human will is done, for better or for worse. And we pray that it be done for better. That our will be in conformity and in accord with God's will. Nature can teach us this. Whenever we pray, "your will be done on Earth as it is in Heaven," we look to that part of Heaven that is closest to us, and

that is nature. Nature can teach us. I remember a passage in Thomas
Merton's diaries where he speaks of watching a sparrow-hawk. In conclusion, he writes: "If only I could be as faithfully a monk as the sparrow-
hawk a sparrow-hawk."

Faithfully is the key word. Earth as God's household will come when
God's will is done faithfully. And faith starts with God, not with us. God's
faithfulness in people is the basis for our faith, a derivative from the same
stem. And our answer is Amen, again from the same stem. Whenever we
say Amen, we respond in faith to the faithfulness of God. Faith is not
belief but trust, trust in God as the ground of being; as Gerard Manley
Hopkins calls it, the "granite shore." The question is not whether God
exists but whether that granite shore, that ground of being, is trustworthy.
Faith is trust in God, or whichever name we give to this ground of being.
Not as potentate, but as unconditional love. God's almighty power is not
the power which can make anything happen. Rather it is the power
which is in us as well, to make whatever happens good and life-giving.
Faith is trust in our true self. As the poet E. E. Cummings says, "I am through
you, so I."

Not only so good, or so beautiful, or so true, but "so I." It is only
through God and in view of God of this ground of being that we are truly
ourselves. Faith is trust in the highest power, the power of love which is
closer to me than I am to myself. Faith is trust in others. Even when we
know that every human is a liar, just as we ourselves are so often unfaithful to ourselves, we still trust. What can that mean? It means that we trust
in that community which unites us with others. It means that we trust
that there is no us and them, we and they anywhere, but all problems are
ours, all solutions are ours, all truth is ours and can become ours through
what one of the Lindisfarne members calls, "detoxifying conversations."
When we speak, when we open ourselves to one another.

Faith is also trust in Earth. Earth as mediation of God's faithfulness.
God's faithfulness at the core of all things. Just as, at the core of a rock,
there is that rock rockness, that embodies and expresses God's faithfulness.
At the core of the oak tree, or of a cherry tree, or of a lilac bush, there is
the faithfulness of oak, cherry, or lilac. At the core of a cat there is catness.
And at the core of a salamander, there is salamanderness. We can rely on
that. And at the core of Gaia is God's love embodied. That is why we can

trust that Gaia also has power to right herself. One of the Lindisfarne Fellows creates living machines, a community of plants and living creatures who detoxify almost any toxin that we humans create. This is simply Earth detoxifying herself.

I know it is not so rosy. I myself live on a fault line in California, and we have earthquakes and other catastrophes. I know that we betray ourselves, our highest ideals, our own true self. I know betrayal by others, cruelty even by friends we deeply trust, and I know that God seems dead at times. And yet faith/trust is our only chance for survival. Without that trust, the worst has already happened. When the son of man comes, will he find faith on Earth? We can turn this question around and ask, can the true human in community come unless faith is found on Earth? And the true human is potentially coming with every child conceived. Will we mediate to those children faithfulness, our own, God's, the Earth's? When the true human comes, will that person find faith on Earth? Our answer must be a commitment, or it will be no answer. And so I would invite you, if you would find it in your hearts to recommit yourselves to God, to your own true selves, to all others, and to Mother Earth.

Here is a pledge all can make: I recommit myself to be faithful to God as I understand God. Amen. I recommit myself to be faithful to my own true self. Amen. I recommit myself to all others. Amen. And I recommit myself to our Mother, the Earth, whose child still to be born is the true human in community, Amen.

October 18, 1992

Clyde's Pickup

WILLIAM BRYANT LOGAN

A year ago, Clyde fell off a scaffold. He is a big Texan, who wears a worn straw cowboy hat, the same jeans every day, and boots that he seems to have been born in.

He had assembled the scaffold out in front of the Great Portal of the Cathedral of St. John the Divine in New York City. He was to check the mortar on some limestone blocks high overhead, lest they come down some Easter morn and clean the bishop's clock while he stood waiting to enter church in the role of the Risen Christ. Somehow, Clyde fell more than forty feet onto grey limestone steps.

While he convalesced in the hospital, his black Chevy pickup truck sat unused and unmoved in a space at the head of the driveway, under a maple tree. The Cathedral's urban pigeon corps has made great, cloud-like white patches of droppings all over it. Inside the cab, between the dashboard and the windshield, are stuffed sheafs and wads of notes, instructions, registrations, a box of toothpicks, casette tapes, catalogues, the tops of commuter coffee cups, stirrers, newspaper clippings, chopsticks, and saw blades. This is Clyde's filing system.

In the back of the pickup lies a rough pile of pigeon-spattered sawed logs, along with a generation of fallen leaves, a broken fanbelt, a yellow empty antifreeze container, numbers of styrofoam cups, a boasted stone, a rusting can of Super Stripe Traffic paint, a few discarded service leaflets and menus for Chinese food, a ticket that reads "admit one," and a vintage book of diocesan records with advertisements for long-vanished vestment stores and Episcopal schools, their lettering now half-eaten by mold.

Out of these leavings a forest is growing. Not on the ground. Not beside the truck. But right in the back of it. The lobes of maple leaves are sharpening as their seedlings sprout, a light and glossy green. The red-stemmed and three-leaved poison ivy is showing its amazing skill at growing out of *any* slightly shady bit of dead wood. (You would think that wood spawned the stuff.) Seeds of albizia have somehow blown from the one little understory specimen halfway down the street and taken hold in the back of the truck. All of this is happening in New York City, fifty yards from Amsterdam Avenue, where the eighteen-wheel trucks whizz by.

In the cab, it's a different story. The dust gathers, the rip in the upholstery creeps infinitesimally toward the back of the seat, the papers yellow and curl. Nothing grows. The "Fan" and the "Hot-Cold" levers remain where they have been for a year. Park-R-D-2-1. Nothing is happening, because the motor is not running.

But in the back of the truck, Great Nature's motor is emphatically running. Left out in the rain, the diocesan book has a sprout in it. The tilted coffee cup has filled with leaf compost, dots of pigeon shit, and wood mold, and albizia is in it. The old black Chevy is alive.

Wherever there are decay and repose, there begins to be soil. It would be hard to imagine a more improbable set of ingredients, but even a truck can become dirt.

How can I stand on the ground every day and not feel its power? How can I live my life stepping on this stuff and not wondering at it? Science says that every gram of soil holds 2.3 horsepower worth of energy. But you could pour gasoline all over the ground forever and never see it sprout maple trees! Even a truck turns to soil. Even an old black pickup.

Recently, I have been reading Exodus, wondering about Moses and the Burning Bush. Moses, it is written, "turns aside to see a wonder," a bush that burns but is not consumed. Throughout my life, I had thought this a ridiculous passage. Why should God get Moses' attention by such outlandish means? I mean, Why couldn't He just have boomed, "Hey, Moses!" the way He would later call to the great king, "Hey, Samuel!"

Now I know why. The truth, when really perceived (not simply described), is always a wonder. Moses does not see a technicolor fantasy. He sees the bush as it really is. He sees the bush as all bushes *actually are.*

There is in biology a formula called the equation of burning. It is half of the fundamental pair of equations by which all organic life subsists. The other half, the equation of photosynthesis, describes the way that plants make foods out of sunlight, carbon dioxide, and water. In the equation of burning, plants (and animals) unlock the stored sunlight and turn it into the heat energy that fuel their motion, their feeling, their thought, or of whatever their living consists.

All that is living burns. This is the fundamental fact of nature. And Moses saw it with his two eyes, directly. That glimpse of the real world—of the world as it is known to God—is not a world of isolated things, but of living processes.

God tells Moses, "Take off your shoes, because the ground where you are standing is Holy Ground." He is asking Moses to experience in his body what the burning bush experiences: a living connection between Heaven and Earth, the life that stretches out like taffy between our father the Sun and our mother the Earth. If you do not believe this, take off your shoes and stand in the grass or in the sand or in the dirt. Just go do it, and I will too!

* IV *

STEWARDSHIP AND RENEWAL

The Third Mediation: The Christian Task of Our Times

THE REV. THOMAS BERRY

Each age of our religious history has its own distinctive work to accomplish. Israel in the prophetic period had its special task to present mankind with a sustaining vision of interpreting present disaster in view of future spiritual transformation. The early Christian ages reconciled the Christian message of redemption with the great cultural traditions of the Greek and Roman worlds. In the medieval period, Christians converted from the incoming barbarian tribes raised up a new civilization out of the ruins of the Roman period. So now we ourselves have a special task to fulfill, the task of renewing the Earth in its primordial florescence after these centuries when humans have devastated the Earth by plundering its resources. This we call the third mediation.

The first mediation is the mediation between the divine and the human, a mediation begun in ancient Israel, continued in the redemption accomplished by Christ, and communicated to the world by the Christian people. This has dominated most of our history. While this preoccupation with the reconciliation between the divine and the human has continued as a central preoccupation of Christian tradition, we have recently given special consideration to the second mediation, the interhuman mediation, the reconciliation of the differing human groups.

With the rise of the industrial establishment, we found our society divided into classes antagonistic to each other. This was also the period when the great nation–states arose. Each was so absolute in its demands that it could not tolerate opposition or injury from any other state. Thus the great international and world conflicts that have arisen with such destructive power over these past two centuries. Thus, too, the great social oppressions and revolutionary movements that have shaken our world.

To deal with this has required special attention to the interhuman mediation as a distinctive aspect of our human and Christian task. This mediation has become ever more urgent in its demands as the human community still spends over a billion dollars each day for military purposes.

Our preoccupation with this second mediation continues even while a third mediation has become an imperative so strong that it overshadows in its significance even this second mediation. I speak of the mediation between the human community and the Earth that surrounds and supports us and upon which we depend in an absolute fashion for the nourishment that sustains us and for every breath that we breathe. In speaking of the Earth I include the sunlight by which all things live, by which we behold the visible things about us, and by which we have the warmth that we need for our survival. Even this sunlight, that comes to us from such a great distance, is communicated to us by the Earth.

It is not only the food for the body that comes from the Earth but our powers of thinking, the great images in our imagination; our arts and our education all proceed from the Earth. Even our knowledge of God comes to us from our acquaintance with the natural world about us. For God has revealed himself first of all in the sky and in the waters and in the wind, in the mountains and valleys, in the birds of the air, and in all those living forms that flower and move over the surface of the planet.

Yet despite this dependence, we have severely damaged the Earth during these past two centuries with our massive technological machines. That these technologies have done much good is surely true; that they have a demonic aspect is also true. We begin to make the Earth a place where the existence of the higher life forms is threatened on a universal scale as we bring about a poisoning of the air, the Earth, and the sea and of all living beings that inhabit these regions of the Earth.

Our urgent task now is to prevent the destruction of the divine image as this is presented to us in the created world, to cease wiping out the sources of our spiritual and intellectual and aesthetic development, to stop the burning away of the irreplaceable resources for foolish and ephemeral purposes. Unless we are totally depraved, we will give to our children not only life and education but a planet with pure air and bright waters and fruitful fields, a planet that can be lived on with grace and beauty, and a touch of human and earthly tenderness.

So far, Christians have not distinguished themselves by their concern for the destinies of the Earth. Now, however, this has become the special role, not only of Christians but of all humankind, a role that no other age could fulfill, a role so important that there may be no other truly human age in the future if the present conflict of humans with the Earth is not resolved, if this role of the third mediation is not fulfilled. The real danger of war in the future is not ultimately that it will destroy such a multitude of human beings but that it might render the Earth inhospitable to life itself in its higher forms. Only the lower forms of the vertebrates and the swarming communities of insects would possess the Earth.

When we turn to examine the resources that Christians possess for fulfilling this task of the third mediation, I would mention first the vast Christian community throughout the world. While Christians have often been estranged from each other in the past, we now begin to reflect on those basic unities that bind us together as a single people. To see this third mediation as the pre-eminent Christian task in our times is to begin formation of a powerful and universal force that hopefully will become effective on the scale that is needed. But even while we speak here of Christian peoples, I would also mention the union of all religious peoples throughout the world who are now concerned with the task of this third mediation.

For this is not simply an economic or political task, bur rather a religious and spiritual task, perhaps the most urgent one of all. Only religious forces can move human consciousness at the depth needed, sustain the effort required over that long period of time during which the adjustment needs to be made, or properly assess the magnitude of what we are about.

Our second spiritual resource is our Christian awareness of the communion to which we are called: communion with the divine source of our being, communion with the entire human community, and, finally, communion with the universe itself. While we have recognized the inseparable nature of the communion with God and with the human community, we have not yet realized that this communion, to be perfected, includes our communion with the Earth and indeed with the entire universe. This is the unique awareness that begins to take place in our times.

That the Body of Christ is ultimately the entire universe is indicated by Saint Paul in the Epistle to the Colossians where he tells us that in Christ "all things hold together." The sacred community ultimately is the entire universe. Neither the incarnation nor the redemption is complete except in this comprehensive context. Only this profound communion with the universe can evoke the energies needed to carry life on into the difficult future.

Christians as well as some of the other great religions of the past have been excessively oriented toward transcendence. A true Earth consciousness needs to be developed. Not only has divine transcendence been such an overwhelming preoccupation, but human transcendence to the natural world has been emphasized. Now we need a greater sense of the human, not as transcendent to the Earth community, but as integral with the Earth community. If God has desired to become a member of the Earth community we should be willing to accept our status as members of this same community.

Our third spiritual resource is the awareness of the creative possibilities of chaos and destruction. That order and beauty and creativity are intimately related to disorder, turmoil, and confusion can be seen from the biblical story of Creation, from the experience of the prophets, from the redemptive sacrifice of Christ, from the emergence of the medieval Christian world out of the dark centuries that followed the decline of Rome. That our times are so destructive forces us to a level of thought and reflection and spiritual renewal such as we might never otherwise attain. It also might presage the shaping of a more resplendent world than we have ever known before.

Our fourth spiritual resource is the sustaining energy that is available to us in our Christian forms of worship, in our ritual, and in our sacraments. This is especially important, for religion is not a sentimental feeling or a pious attitude or an escape from the real challenge of life. It is rather a way of dealing with the hard and difficult and threatening moments of life and with the terrors of death. No other force has yet been discovered that can so sustain us in adversity, so inspire us in our moments of exaltation, or so awaken the imaginative and creative forces within us.

Nor is religion a stiff, unyielding fixation made for some other age, or some other place, or for some other issues other than those we face at the present time. Religion is, rather, as adaptable as life itself. It is as real as the Earth we stand on, as present as the air we breathe. Christian faith particularly includes not only faith in God, but faith in the human community, and faith in the natural world. Religion rectifies not by domination but by invocation. This is the attitude and the power that we need. Indeed our difficulties have been caused principally by a certain distrust of the Earth and by a managerial mania that seeks to replace or manipulate the marvelous variety and interlacing of the intimate life forces of nature with mechanistic processes and chemical concoctions that are ultimately ruinous to the entire biosphere, the great web of life that encircles the Earth. A new confidence in the Earth is needed along with a new capacity for communion with the Earth. Only through communion can we have community. Only through an integral community can we survive.

In conclusion, I would suggest that the fulfillment of this third mediation, the establishment of a harmonious relation between humans and the Earth, may well be the origin of a more effective interhuman mediation and even lead to a more perfect divine–human mediation. I might note, finally, that our lenten season is not merely a religious or human ritual. It has its ultimate origin in a profound annual Earth-renewal process. The redemptive sacrifice of Christ was, from the beginning, understood within this springtime renewal experience.

We do not then proceed with our renewal celebration simply by our own human initiative. We are inspired and sustained by the powers of Heaven and Earth which are present to us in our eucharistic liturgy. A new stage of interaction between the divine, the natural, and the human is begun. Hopefully we will carry it through to completion for our own sakes but even more for the sake of our children. The world before us is their world even more than it is our world. If we have damaged it in the past, the time has come for the great healing. This is the historical task of our times.

1982

The Church as Renewed Creation

THE REV. JEFFREY GOLLIHER

It has become clear that the ultimate success or failure of the 1992 Earth Summit in Rio de Janeiro is tied up as much with the churches and what the churches do, as it is with the behavior of nations around the world. We look ahead into the future with great hope. And as we look ahead, we notice a great contrast, perhaps a contrast never so great in history, a contrast betwen the beauty and wonder of Creation and the darkness and failure of the world. On the one hand, people realize more and more that the planet is, in fact, an interdependent whole. On the other, the political borders between nations more and more become walls of fear and bigotry. These walls profoundly deny the higher truth of our common humanity and our common home on Earth.

Today, we are beginning to reclaim an ancient truth about the Church: our temple, our true place of worship, is the Earth itself. Our church buildings, including this Cathedral, are symbolic of this larger truth, pointing to the reality of the greater whole of the Earth. Let there be no mistake about it—the Church in its greater meaning and its deeper mystery is ultimately God's Creation in the process of renewal.

This ancient vision of the Church is still a dream, as it was almost two thousand years ago. It is still a dream today, but that should neither lessen our hope nor obscure our belief in the power of dreaming, because the challenge we have before us is urgent and imperative. At times like today, it is good to remember the words of Thomas Berry when he speaks of "the Dream of the Earth," or Verna Dozier, when she talks about "the Dream of God"—and then we know that when we dream together, we're in good company.

My work and my ministry—and of course almost the entire ministry of the Cathedral of St. John the Divine—is devoted in one way or another to this dream: to work with other people throughout the city, in the Northeast, and all across the planet in order to do everything we can to make the Church as renewed Creation into a living reality. Whether we're working with homeless people, or people with AIDS, or restoring salt marshes, the mission of St. John the Divine is the same, each ministry forming one part of an integral vision of Creation renewed. Our vision embraces all our relationships—with God and with Creation—because our ecological vision includes human nature too. As creatures, we are part of Creation; our existence binds us intricately with the origin and fate of the Earth.

Yet, our experience is not always that straightforward or simple. Sometimes, we become almost frozen because our collective hope and mission seem too large. We become overwhelmed by the immensity of it all and by the magnitude of what we have to do now and in the near future. The ecological clock is ticking, and we know it.

We all know about this feeling of frozen helplessness. Our global environmental crisis has a very real spiritual and psychological and emotional side to it, and it would be a grave mistake to deny feelings that are uncertain or ambiguous—because in all the uncertainty, there is real struggle, and when struggle exists, then the opportunity for growth exists as well. It's a fact that when we speak about the environment in church or at home or school—it doesn't matter where—when we talk about poverty and disease, ozone depletion, toxic wastes, and the rest of it—at those times, we are speaking to some of the greatest hopes and to some of the deepest fears that people have ever imagined in all of human history. And it's for that reason, in these overwhelming times, that we need to be very thoughtful and prayerful about the gospel story that we tell and share with each other.

Consider the very architecture of the Cathedral of St. John the Divine. In this vast, expansive, holy place we can understand—through the Spirit and through our senses—that the whole planet, like this Cathedral, is one interconnected whole. Here and in places like this, the feeling of frozen helplessness becomes much smaller and our hearts open, almost naturally, to the even more overwhelming mystery of God. We're reminded that there is unity; there is a pattern that weaves all of us together with a sacred bond. St. Paul in his Epistle to the Colossians, says, quite boldly, that the connecting pattern is Christ. He is the "image of the invisible God, the firstborn of all Creation. . . . He himself is before all things, and in him all things hold together."

Christ's Spirit is a living presence in the Cathedral. Above the high altar you can see Christ represented in the mostly red stained glass window. This is the Christ who is the source of our interconnected existence, but even more, he is the way that we will rediscover our relationship to God the Creator—perhaps today, or someday in the future. It's overwhelming when we let ourselves be captured by the vision, by the dream. This experience of being overwhelmed lies, ultimately, at a place very close to the center of our being: it's at the heart of our dream of the Church, and it's part of the spiritual message we want to remember and pass on to others, and to our children.

A second, equally important mesage, has to do with our purpose in God's Creation and our responsibility. In effect, God says, "I made you and everything else; and all of it is good. Your job is to look after things, and to be good stewards." Our responsibiltiy is not to rip apart the unity which Christ already holds together, but to help preserve the integrity of Creation and the integrity of people.

What this means is that knowing who we are as individuals and as groups of people and knowing that we are a part of Creation, is more important than knowing which side we're on in any given controversy. This magnificent Cathedral—as large as it is—is still a relatively small scale model of the cosmos. Are there any sides to take here, sides to choose? No, there are no sides to take in the Creation that Christ holds together. And this also means that no one—not one person, not one small part of Creation, not even the darker and hidden parts of ourselves that we like to forget—nothing is left out. We make different choices, yes, and we don't all agree about everything, but in the deepest parts of our soul and in the broadest planetary way, we're all in this together.

When we open our hearts and begin to "dream of the church," we start to feel and see the unity of God's Creation, but that's only part of the story. Having even a glimpse of how Christ holds all things together is not enough. There's another, more important part of our dream, and that part, in all likelihood, is the major stumbling block facing us together. Often this stumbling block is discussed with the respect to the words "dominion" and "subdue" found in the Creation account of Genesis.

These words have been applied wrongly in recent history to justify exploiting the environment. But the real issue at stake in all this controversy is really "control" and the belief that everything will work out for the best, if only we could better control things, control other people, and even control experience itself.

I saw this control issue come to the surface very recently at the White Mountain School, a small Episcopalian school in New England. The school had asked the Cathedral to help them become a place of environmental education for high-school-age students. And so, I put together a plan for how they might accomplish what they want to do. At a meeting of the board of trustees, when we were all thinking over the plan and related matters, one of the board members, after a rather long period of pensive silence, spoke up. He said: "It seems to me that to be a truly ecological school we are going to have to give up believing that we're in control of everything." He was being truthful and straightforward. This was the one person in the room that I would have least expected to say that—and I was just surprised. The point, of course, is that he was and is exactly right, and as he spoke, people knew that something beautiful was happening inside this man, although not everyone understood the depth of his truth, and some of the people there probably thought he was a little crazy.

Among other things, he discovered that he is not the one who holds all things together—Christ does. And this too, is the Christ who can cause quite a stir, to say the least, and some discomfort in our souls, making it seem that the world is not coming together at all, but falling apart. This is the Christ who became incarnate in human form, in a body, in space and time, and in a particular place, with a family and friends. And this Christ made some enemies—although those enemies were not his own.

To find who we are as people, and as Christians, we need both stories. We need the Christ who holds together, and we need the Christ who seems to rip apart—especially when we forget that not we, but God is in control of the universe. The real temptation we face in all this is to believe that our task as Christians is to merge with the oneness, without facing up to our responsibilites in the here and now. Christ came to show us the way of holy living on Earth, and what that way is like is described in Luke's Gospel reading today. The passage is sometimes called "the gospel within the Gospel," because it encapsulates so much that's at the heart of our faith.

Jesus is nailed to the cross. First the accusing crowd, and then one of the others being crucified, say to Jesus, "Are you not the Messiah? Save yourself and us." This is real temptation—save yourself, use your power, and take control of the situation. You're the center of all things, after all; take some control! Today, in the United States, we know quite a lot about this temptation of false power. We recognize it in the belief that our ticket to Heaven is to control nature and consume more resources; in the notion that Heaven is a reward for our own achievements on Earth (which implies that we control the price of admission); and in the belief that the control of women by men, or the control of one race by another, is a right and holy thing to do. We recognize it, too, in the belief that children are our possessions, rather than God's. All these arise from the misguided assumption that we are the ones in control of the Spirit. Let's face it: there is no servanthood, no humility, no discipleship, no stewardship in any of this.

Jesus rejected this temptation of false power. Instead, he took the form of a servant. This is what he wants us to do too! In that very act and by his example, he shows us two things: he shows us how to live, and he shows us who we are. He demonstrates plainly, for everyone to see, what the holy scripture means when it says that people are made in the image of God. We become God's image, when we become servants of others, servants of truth, servants of God's Creation—and when we do that, we also become fully human.

Does this mean that we are something other than the crown of God's Creation? No, but it does mean that the real crown of Creation is the steward of Creation, and anything else is a spiritual dead-end and an environmental disaster. Our place in nature is defined by our responsibility to care for it and each other, rather than by how nature and others might be useful to us. Ecology teaches us that prayerfulness is a doorway to renewed Creation, when we give ourselves over to God in self-emptying worship.

So, we have a challenge, and the challenge has its rewards. Let go of our obsession with control, and learn how to live. Give up the pursuit of power over others, and so strengthen our souls. Forsake claiming power over Creation, and enter a deeper relationship with Christ. Christ is the one who holds all things together—and with our help, with our actions, and with our dream of the Church, he, ultimately, is the one who will renew God's Creation.

November 22, 1992

Making Security Profitable

AMORY B. LOVINS

In Borneo in the early 1950s, the Dayak people suffered from malaria, and the World Health Organization had a solution: they would simply spray DDT all over. They did, the mosquitoes died, the malaria declined; so far, so good, but there were many side effects. The roofs of people's houses, for example, began to fall down on their heads, because the DDT had also killed tiny parasitic wasps that had previously controlled thatch-eating caterpillars. Then the DDT-poisoned bugs were eaten by geckoes, which were eaten by cats. As the DDT built up in the food chain, it killed the cats. Without the cats, the rats flourished and multipled. The World Health Organization was threatened by outbreaks of typhus and plague, which it had itself created, and was thereby obliged to parachute live cats into Borneo.

This true parable of Operation Cat Drop—courtesy of the British Royal Air Force—nicely illustrates how, if we don't know how things are connected, often the cause of problems is solutions. If we do know how things are connected, we can often make the cause of solutions be solutions: we can solve one problem in a way that also solves many others without making more—before we have to parachute more cats.

There is much to be retaught. Our country, like most countries, has many needs and doesn't know how to pay for them. If, as Abba Eban said, "People and nations behave wisely—once they have exhausted all other alternatives," we have certainly been working our way well down the list. The very gifts whose unwise use has brought us so close to ruin now offer new opportunities to redirect much of our effort from squandering to rebuilding, from destroying to creating, from spending to cultivating, and from getting to giving.

This morning, I will sketch a few parts of a rich tapestry of new ways to create a society in which succeeding generations can achieve a better quality of life—a society we might call "secure," because *security*, says the dictionary, is "freedom from fear of privation or attack." Only when those two interlinked fears, and the costs incurred to keep them at bay, cease to dominate our consciousness—only when we can be safe and feel safe, in ways that work better and cost less than present arrangements—can we focus our social energies on worthy goals.

In the past, security meant tanks and military intelligence. Today, security is more about super-efficient cars and civilian intelligence. In the past, security meant naval guns; today, it means caulk guns. In the past, security came from the threat or use of institutionalized violence, and was a monopoly of national governments. Today, security comes from making others more secure, not less, and it is the province of every citizen. In the past, security was costly, but today it can be profitable enough to pay for many social needs we had deemed unaffordable.

The key to this happy result is harnessing the hidden connections within how we think about a secure society and how we achieve it. For the forty-five years of the Cold War, we thought of security simply as military strength. Appended and subordinated to it was a militarized economic policy, devoting most of our science and technology to weaponry, and a militarized energy and resource policy, in which the way to get others' resources was to take them. Environmental concerns were ignored, and indeed derided as an obstacle to economic strength. But today, we are starting to see the economic, environmental, energy and resource, and military elements of security as the four points of a tetrahedraon—an immensely strong structure if its four vertices are firmly connected.

Energy is central to many of these connections:

- We recently fought—indeed, are still fighting—a war over oil. Even in peacetime, America spends upwards of fifty billion dollars a year on military forces to intervene in the Persian Gulf—four times what we pay for the oil itself, which in turn is a tiny fraciton of its replacement value. We recently put our kids in half-a-mile-per-gallon tanks and seventeen-feet-per-gallon aircraft carriers because we didn't put them in thirty-two-mile-per-gallon cars. That's all it would have taken, if we'd done nothing else, to eliminate oil imports from the Persian Gulf. And although there was more at stake in the Gulf War than just oil, it's hard to believe we'd have put a half-million troops there if Kuwait just grew broccoli.

- Overuse and misuse of energy is the primary cause of urban smog, acid rain, global warming, and endangered oceans.

- Energy use bleeds the conomy. Oil imports alone have accounted for nearly three-fourths of the United States' trade deficit since 1970—a one trillion dollar transfer of wealth from our streets to OPEC nations. The hemorrhage of both direct and military dollars for foreign oil costs American jobs by not being spent and invested at home. The lack of investment then keeps us inefficient and dependent. It's a vicious circle.

Yet that costly addition to foreign oil, and its constraints on our foreign and military policy, are a problem we don't need to have, and it's cheaper not to. If we'd simply kept on saving oil as fast after 1985 as we did for the previous nine years, we wouldn't have needed a drop of oil from the Persian Gulf since then. Instead, dumb policies increased Gulf imports by sixfold since 1985.

Oil is used in many ways, including heating the Cathedral of St. John the Divine, and most of it can be saved in every case. New superwindows that insulate as well as six or even twelve sheets of glass, for example, can save twice as much oil and gas as we get from Alaska, cheaper than we can drill for more; such windows in my own house let us grow five banana crops the winter before last with no furnace, while outside temperatures dipped below -40 degrees.

But the key is, of course, cars. Light vehicles use two-fifths of all the oil we burn. We drive inefficient (and increasingly foreign-made) cars, burning foreign oil, across crumbling bridges, into traffic jams in smoggy cities. What we should be doing instead is reinvesting those oil dollars to pay American autoworkers to make super-efficient, clean cars, and to pay American contractors to rebuild our infrastructure. That can turn the vicious circle into a virtuous circle of saved money, jobs, health, environment, and national security. It changes our nation from inefficient and dependent to efficient and independent.

Consider General Motors. The world's largest corporation, directly and indirectly touching a sixth of all Americans, has been losing touch, losing market, losing money, and laying off people. But there's another side of the story. A year and a half ago, a few dozen brilliant GM craftspeople and engineers spent the equivalent of about eight hours' North American losses to build a doubled-efficiency four-passenger sports car. Their Ultralite can carry four adults safely and comfortably coast to coast on twenty-nine gallons of gas, cruising at one hundred miles per gallon on 3.4 horsepower. It has over a hundred significant innovations. They built it in one hundred days. And other companies can do it too.

That carbon fiber concept car is the forerunner of a new breed of ultralight electric-hybrid cars that can achieve about 150 mpg soon and probably 300 ultimately. That's for a safe, comfortable, clean, beautiful, durable, quiet, family car. What will such a "supercar" cost? Probably about the same as today's cars and quite possibly less. And America leads in all the technologies needed to do it. That would recreate Detroit as the world market leader—and simultaneously slash oil imports, clean up urban air, and dampen global warming. It's one of the most important ways to use innovations in the domestic economy to create energy, military, and environmental security and make money on the deal.

Coming at us rapidly is a fundamental transformation in the car industry, as in many others. Foresight can give us vibrant, world-leading automakers. Continued drift can give us collapsed, uncompetitive automakers. If we want automaking jobs in America, we need to start serious work now on making a graceful transition. How will we pay for the retraining and retooling? Let's start by investing in our own people and factories that fifty billion dollars a year we're now spending on imported oil to blow out those tailpipes.

To get supercars off the drawing boards and into the showrooms, we don't have to get stuck in the sterile rhetoric of high gasoline taxes vs. stiff Federal efficiency standards. There are other options for unleashing American entrepreneurship. For example, California's legislature passed by a 7:1 margin two years ago—though it was vetoed after the session—

the "Drive+" proposal. Under this "feebate," when you buy a car, you pay a fee or get a rebate; which and how big depends on how efficient it is (and perhaps also how clean and safe it is); and the fees pay for the rebates. We could even tie rebates for efficient cars to the difference in efficiency between the new car you buy and the old car you scrap. This would get good cars on the road and bad cars off the road much faster—great news for Detroit (which could sell lots more cars), for American jobs, and for getting the oil, air, and climate benefits far sooner.

Other innovative policies, many being invented in New York, can help all transportation and land-use alternatives to compete fairly, reducing unnecessary travel and congestion. This is essential, because efficient cars only buy time; they don't solve the basic problem of personal transportation and livable cities. If we had clean, safe, renewably fueled, 150 mpg station wagons, then two billion Chinese or ten million Los Angeleans or eight million New Yorkers driving them still wouldn't work; we wouldn't run out of oil or air, but we'd run out of roads and patience.

Avoiding the constraints du jour will require sensible land use in which people are already pretty much where they want to be, so they're not always trying to get someplace else, and we'll need cities where walking, biking, and public transit really work, so we aren't isolating the old and the young, giving up the public realm to hurtling steel boxes, and reducing our social interactions to aggressive competition for squares of asphalt.

Cleaning up the air and protecting the Earth's climate needn't cost more; in fact it can be highly profitable if we do it mainly through energy efficiency, because today it's generally cheaper to save fuel than to burn fuel. By substituting efficiency for fuel, we reduce pollution and not at a cost but at a profit—and, being profitable, this can be done in the market. That's why America's third-largest electric utility has given away more than a million compact fluorescent lamps: it's cheaper to give you a quadrupled-efficiency lamp than just to fuel existing power plants. Each lamp, over its life, avoids putting into the air a ton of carbon dioxide, twenty pounds of sulfur oxide, and other pollutants; but far from costing extra, it creates tens of dollars of net wealth. And that wealth can benefit everyone. Such lamps can cut by a fifth the evening peak load that crashes the grid in Bombay; they can increase a North Carolina chicken grower's profits by one-fourth; in a very poor country like Haiti, they may increase disposable household income by as much as one-third. And this is one of the smaller and costlier efficiency opportunties available.

Indeed, saving electricity is even more lucrative than saving oil, because it costs about six to eight times as much. And each unit of saved electricity saves three to four units of fuel, mainly coal, at the power plant, so it has huge leverage in reducing global warming and acid rain.

It's great news that new American technologies now on the market, if well and fully applied to existing buildings and equipment, could save most of the electricity we now use, far more cheaply than just running our coal and nuclear power plants, even if building those plants cost nothing. For example, recent experience, some of it in New York, confirms that we can cost-effectively save about three-fourths of the energy used in existing offices, shops, and homes, while providing even better services. A few months ago, a California office retrofit saved 93 per cent of air-conditioning energy while improving comfort; last year, Boeing saved 90 per cent of its lighting energy while letting its people see better (and hence make better aircraft) and making its plants look better. Every developer, landlord, tenant, and homeowner in New York deserves an opportunity to apply these new methods.

Utilities, including ConEd, are now starting to help by financing billions of dollars worth of their customers' efficiency improvements every year. As more states change their regulations so utilities get rewarded not for selling more energy but for cutting your bills, many utilities are aggressively clearing away the barriers to efficiency. The nation's largest private utility now says it will get at least three-fourths of its new power needs in the '90s from efficiency. That's what happens when we let utilities take economics seriously and chooose the best buys first.

Such "least-cost" investments have huge leverage not only for a cleaner environment but also for good jobs in a healthy economy. For example, just designing our buildings and air-conditioning equipment properly could displace up to a trillion dollars' worth of unnessary investments— no sweat. Think what that kind of reinvestment could do to rebuild America. And the same new ways to finance, market, and deliver energy savings can also be adapted to many other kinds of resource savings— including the water efficiency that could, if begun now, do much to prevent the next war in the Middle East.

Energy and resource efficiency can also work directly to make our businesses far more competitive One big aerospace company, for example, expected its investment in daylighting a big design building to pay back in seven years; but people loved the natural light so much that absenteeism fell by 15 per cent. The resulting higher productivity not only paid off the investment in one year, it also enabled the company to win a tough contract—whose profits then paid for the entire building! Similarly, when the biggest independent maker of rod, wire, and cable saved 40 per cent of the electricity and 60 per cent of the natural gases used to make a pound of product, its lower energy bill produced all its profits during a tough time when many of its competititors went under. The two engineers who achieved those savings may have saved four thousand jobs at ten plants in six states.

Saved energy dollars especially boost the economy of our own communities. In Osage, Iowa, helping the four thousand people with basic savings like weatherization enabled the town's utility to prepay all its debts; build up a multimillion dollar cash reserve; cut the rates five times in five years, to only half the Iowa average, thereby attracting two big factories to town and keeping the existing ones competitive in tough global markets; and most importantly, keep over one thousand dollars per household per year—money that had previously gone out of town to buy utility inputs—recirculating in the local economy, supporting local jobs and local multipliers, and making Osage noticeably more prosperous than comparable towns nearby. If a healthy Wall Street starts on Main Street, Osage is an apt model for our future.

Indeed, energy efficiency is already saving the United States $150 billion a year. But that just scratches the surface of what's now available and worthwhile. Getting as efficient as Germany and Japan would save an *additional* $200 billion a year; getting as efficient as they should be now would raise our savings to about $300 billion a year. So just using energy in a way that saves money could save America about as much as the Federal budget deficit, or about as much as the entire military budget of the thousand dollars a second—simultaneously unhooking us from Mideast oil, saving the environment, and making jobs: over a million net new jobs by 2010. Over the next few decades, an energy-efficient America could save trillions of dollars—as much as the national debt.

The Energy Security Act signed in October 1992 does little to save oil; it reflects the outmoded view that the best response to domestic oil depletion is to deplete faster. But drilling for oil in our underinsulated attics, our inefficient cars, and our uncompetitive factories is the best single way to rebuild America's strength from within. Just the supergiant oilfield saved by scrapping Petropigs and Brontomobiles is bigger than the biggest in Saudi Arabia; it's cheaper than drilling anywhere else, it doesn't pollute, it can't be cut off, and it'll never run out.

Already the millions of little things we've all done to save energy in the past twenty years have added up to a new national energy source two-fifths bigger than the entire domestic oil industry. That's why, by 1985, we'd cut total oil imports in half, and cut Gulf imports by over 90 per cent from their peak. But several times that much still remains to be saved. And efficiency is the key to switching to energy sources that don't run out—sources that, government studies show, could cost-effectively provide about half our present total energy use and all our electric use by 2030, well within the life of a nonrenewable power plant ordered today.

Energy and resource efficiency directly puts dollars back in your pocket. It helps poor people the most, because they spend the largest proportion of their income on energy. It has all the stimulative effect of a middle-class tax cut, but it lowers, not raises the federal deficit. Energy efficiency is not only one of the new pillars of security, it's also the fastest, surest, fairest, and most broadly beneficial way to get the economy moving.

But while a best-buys-first energy policy will create jobs, rebalance trade, cut pollution, and free up hundreds of billions of dollars of scarce domestic capital, it cannot restore our nation to prosperity by itself.

A coherent economic strategy is also needed—starting by rejecting the myth that we can be rich or clean, but not both. On the contrary, our competitiveness lags in part because American companies produce five times as much waste per dollar of goods sold as the Japanese, and twice that of the Germans. Pollution means wasted resources. It means you're wasting money on energy, water, and materials you don't need—and wasting money on pollution control, incinerators, landfills, illnesses, lawsuits, and fines.

Germany and Japan have some of the world's strictest environmental laws and highest energy prices. Those conditions helped drive industrial innovation on a broad front, yielding world-class resource efficiency, low waste, strong economies, and trade surpluses. Indeed, a booming sector of their economies sell or license pollution-control, energy-saving, and recycling equipment to America. Similarly, within the United States, those states with stronger environmental policies consistently outperform the weaker environmental states on all measures of economic results. Until we charge ourselves what environmental harm really costs, we won't know how much is enough, and will continue to throw our resources "away" in the false belief that there is an "away" to throw them—not just a boomerang practice range.

A national economic strategy shouldn't be aimed at picking winners and losers, at shielding industries from competition, but rather at improving the competitiveness and efficiency of all industries. Such policies are nothing new; they created many of today's most dynamic industries, like aerospace and computers. But such military–industrial policy, with its slow spinoff of research and development to civilian technologies, became increasingly ineffective in a world of newly reconstructed and vibrant economic competitors. Today both Germany and Japan spend much more of their wealth on civilian R and D than does the United States. Germany outinvests the U.S. on worker training by 4:1. Japan outinvests us in infrastructure by 3:1. So it's not surprising that we have lost three million manufacturing jobs since 1979, that median family income is now lower than it was twenty years ago, and that we are the only major industrialized nation whose manufacturing workers earn less per hour than a decade ago. We simply underinvest and misinvest relative to our competititors.

That is why we need to take the money saved by smarter military spending and desubsidizing energy and use it to restore funding for civilian R and D in critical technologies (emphasizing lean/clean/green production), for resource-efficient infrastructure, and for training, especially for the 75 per cent of the work force who lack a college degree—the same people whose living standards have fallen for the past fifteen years. We should consider an apprentice training system somewhat like Germany's industry/government system—a key reason Germany has the highest-paid workers and the lowest level of youth unemployment in Europe. And we must improve U.S. manufacturing, lest investments in new technology only create jobs abroad, as it has in the past with consumer electronics.

America is the world's leading exporter of agricultural products, in large part because of an extension program to provide farmers access to new technology and training. Manufacturing is ten times as big as agriculture, but today's tiny program to diffuse new manufacturing technologies to small businesses gets less than one-tenth the funding of Ag Extension.

These ideas suggest why the first post-Cold-War administration has a unique opportunity to put in place a new vision of national security and to restore America's prosperity. The end of the Cold War presents ideal starting points: to adopt a market-oriented energy policy, to demilitarize economic policy, to practice sustainable environmental policy, and to integrate all three.

Yet, that's the easy part. It's just the beginning of healing our society, creating justice, and reversing the war against the Earth. To do that, we'll have to rethink fundamentally our relationship to the Creation, to our own capacities and purposes, and to our children. Our miraculous technological cleverness needs a hefty dose of Gaian wisdom. Two questions especially echo from the turbulence of the 1980s: the difference between ecology and engineering, and the difference between economics and human purpose.

It is one of nature's rules that those who don't play by the rules won't play at all. Yet too many of us think in the very different terms of old physical science. As a physicist, I was trained to think of the macroscopic world as acting a lot like billiard balls. That's risky in a biological and social world whose complex systems often behave nonlinearly and chaotically. Moreover, the power of the physical sciences: successes invites *hubris*. It reinforces manipulative technologies meant to bend nature to our will, or even to supplant nature altogether. It misleads us to think of the awesome living world as an inconvenience to be evaded rather than as model and mentor. It makes us suppose we know most of the Book of Life, not just the first few pages. It makes most of our farming and forestry practices into soil-mining. It makes us treat soil like dirt, living things as dead, nature as nuisance, billions of years' worth of design experience as casually discardable, and the future as worthless (at a ten percent real discount rate). It leads us to develop ever more dangerous tools—first nuclear fission, then genetic engineering, now nanotechnology—tools that are suitable, as Robert Sinsheimer warned, only "for a wise, farseeing, and incorruptible people."

Moreover, imitating the precise, mechanistic style that modern physics has long abandoned, has spawned a swarm of economic theorists preoccupied with what's countable rather than with what counts. Seduction by the simple theoretical model of market behavior has caused widespread economic fundamentalism and moral blindness. A noted World Bank economist recently advised, apparently intending no offense, that hazardous processes and toxic wastes be put among the world's poor, because then the lower wages lost if anyone were thereby killed or injured would depress global economic output less.

Economic output in turn is a bizarre way of expressing the sum of human happiness or even of material satisfaction: it is simply a sum of the market value of goods, services, bads, and nuisances sold for money, excluding everything that has no price (such as serving and caring) and everything that is priceless. Economic output, too, simply reflects the extent and speed of a supposedly endless, disembodied flow of exchange value, looping perpetually around between production and consumption—as if the economic process weren't also embedded in a flow of physical resources from depletion to pollution. Economist Herman Daly says it's like trying to understand an animal in terms only of its circulatory system, without noticing that it also has a digestive tract that ties it firmly to its environment at both ends. And in a widely condoned and systematic theft from the future, the depletion and pollution are generally assumed to cost nothing, however dearly they may cost our kids. As Hugh Nash remarked, how can we better pay tribute to our descendents' boundless technological ingenuity than to make sure they'll need it? In the past dozen years, market economics became no less than the U.S. state religion, to which forecasts were aligned, praises sung, and goats sacrificed daily. Why did the outgoing administration so adamantly oppose any action to abate climatic change? Because, their eminent theorist claimed, it would cost some $200 billion a year. How so? Well, according to economic theory, using energy more efficiently must not be cost-effective, or people would have done it already; so obviously inducing them to do so much requires huge energy taxes that would depress output. What about extensive, carefully measured utility and industry data showing that energy efficiency is highly cost-effective but has been retarded by well-known market failures—so the calculation of a $200-billion-a-year saving?

Well, that's an interesting hypothesis, the distinguished economists replied, but we'll stick with our nice theory—as if they lay awake nights worrying about whether what works in practice could possibly work in theory. They added that anyhow, global warming matters only to agriculture, which is only 2 per cent of GNP—as if we could eat economic theories, or your heart didn't matter because it's only 2 per cent of your body weight. God save us from such ninnies.

Markets are a valuable short-term way to allocate scarce resources. But markets never tell us how much is enough, or when legitimate needs are being subordinated to extravagant wants. As Herman Daly notes, "A boat that is loaded with too much weight will sink, even if the weight is optimally allocated." That's not news: Ecclesiastes reminded us that "He that hath silver shall not be satisfied with silver, nor he that hath abundance with increase, this is also vanity." But to most economists, it is also a Grosser National Product, so it is good. As Lewis Mumford wrote, it turns all of the Seven Deadly Sins into positive virtues—except sloth—and that's supposedly good, too.

Our public discourse about economic goals will continue to substitute empty slogans for real values until we remember, in Dana Meadows's words, that "A sustainable society would be interested in qualitative development, not physical expansion. It would use material growth as a considered tool, not a perpetual mandate. It would be neither for nor against growth. Rather, it would begin to discriminate kinds of growth and purposes for growth. Before this society would decide on any specific growth proposal, it would ask what the growth is for, who would benefit, what it would cost, how long it would last, and whether it could be accommodated by the sources and sinks of the planet." I believe the uneasy American people are hungry for leaders who ask those questions—leaders who, as Robert Gilman urges, extend the Golden Rule through time, doing unto future generations of living beings as we would have done unto us.

American public life offers a myriad recent examples of basic confusions between the creation of wealth and the pursuit of happiness; between profit opportunities and basic rights; between private gains and public goals. After all, economic efficiency is only a means, not an end. Markets are meant to be efficient, not sufficient; greedy, not fair. Markets were never meant to achieve community or integrity, beauty or justice, sustainability or sacredness—and they don't. If markets do something good for whales or wilderness or God or Gaia or grandchildren, that's purely coincidental. Markets are very good at achieving their stated goals, but those goals are far from the whole purpose of a human being. It's to seek that fuller purpose that we have politics, ethics, and religion; and if we ever suppose these can be replaced by economics, we stand in peril of our souls.

Mullah Nasrudin was once asked which is more valuable, the Moon or the Sun. "Why, the Moon!" he replied—"because it shines at night, when we need the light more." Today, too, we need the light more. May each of us find that light in plenty as your people, in the weeks and years ahead, begin the renewal of our polity and our spirituality.

January 17, 1993

Design for Renewal

WILLIAM MCDONOUGH

As part of his eulogy to Archbishop Louis Kahn, Vincent Scully described crossing the Red Square with Kahn. In his excited way, he'd looked at Lou and said, "Isn't it wonderful the way the domes of St. Basil's Cathedral reach up into the sky?" Kahn had replied, "Isn't it beautiful the way they come down to the ground?"

I want to look at design as a signal of the intention of a human being: of how the things we make must rise from the ground and how they must return to it. Start with ecology. Ecology comes from the Greek roots, *ecos* and *logos*, "household" and "discourse." First we have to look at our planet and understand how it works. Essentially, we can see there are fundamental characteristics that are in natural design that we can use as models and mentors for our own work.

One is the stuff of it: the stones, the clay, the wood. The putty of our work is already here. Everything we have to work with is already here. We can see there is this glow that is this putty. We see that, within that and withon it, waste equals food. In nature, there is no such thing as waste except at the level of species. Everything is cycled constantly through nature. There is no such thing as waste.

The second thing which we realize is that the thing that allows life to exist is the one thing that comes from outside of this system: perpetual solar income.

The third thing we realize is that we have an astonishing amount of diversity. People talk about biodiversity, but there is diversity of every kind. That's what allows the system (which is always highly complex, always verging on chaos) to exist and maintain itself. In this light we can look at the notion of economy as coming from the same root. How well are we measuring our work? Gross National Product measurements don't seem to make much sense any more. If we look at GNP-type measurements of Valdez, Alaska, we find that it's been doing awfully well. There are so many people there cleaning up. So what are we measuring, and have we put our natural resources on the asset side of a ledger? We haven't and we must.

As a designer, I want to put these fundamental revelations about waste equals food, current solar income, and protecting biodiversity, into my work. The way I'd like to start looking at that is to reflect upon a comment of Emerson. In 1831, when his wife died, he went to Europe on a sailboat and returned on a steamship. He remarked on the return voyage that he missed the "Aolean Kinetic." In other words, he went over on a solar-powered recyclable vehicle operated by craftspersons working in the open air, practicing ancient arts. He returned in a steel rust bucket, spilling oil on the waters, smoking to the sky, operated by people in a black dungeon shoveling coal into the mouth of a boiler. Both these ships were objects of design. These objects were designed by people.

Peter Senge at MIT's Sloan School of Management runs a Learning Laboratory about how organizations learn. The very first question he asks of CEO's who come there is "Who is the leader on a ship crossing the ocean?" He gets such answers as you can imagine: Captain, Navigator, Helmsman, Chefs. He says, "No, the leader of the ship is the designer of the ship. Because everyone on that ship is the effect of its design. The trouble is we are still designing steamships. We are still designing things that work from fossil fuels and have deleterious effects. We need a new sort of design. We need to design a boat for Thoreau. This is a great challenge because Thoreau never wanted to leave Walden Pond. When asked why he never traveled, he said, "I traveled widely in Concord."

I grew up in the Far East and when I came to this country as an American, I was shocked. It seemed that we no longer had people with lives in America. Instead, it seems we have consumers with lifestyles. When did we stop having people? Television news always talks about consumers, not people.

We are people with lives. Let us think about the making of things. If I am a consumer, what can I consume? Shoe polish, food, liquid, toothpaste? I cannot consume a television set. Why are we creating systems of stress where people can be presumed to consume a television set? If you think about it, if I put a TV set here and covered it up with this robe and say, "I have this amazing item. What it will do as a service will astonish you. Before I tell you what it does, let me tell you what it is and you tell me if you want this in your house. It has 4,060 chemicals, eighteen grams of highly toxic mercury, it has an explosive glass tube, and we think you ought to put it eye-level with children and encourage them to play with it." That is a television set.

One ecological chemist has suggested that we remove the word *waste* from our vocabulary and start using the word *product* instead. Let's think about the three kinds of products. First, there are consumer products. We should be throwing our banana peels into our gardens, to restore the health of our soil. Shampoos should be in bottles that would be biodegradable and would go into compost. It should be shipped without a lot of water, plastics, heavy metals, and dyes. We should create serious consumer goods that actually are consumed to go back to the soil.

The second-tier product is the television set, for example. It is a service product. Sony should lease you the television set. It belongs to them. What gives you the right to consume a TV? You can walk down the street, dump it in a garbage can and walk away, bringing persistent poisoning all over the planet. Why should we give people with lives that responsibility and that stress? If you put twenty of them in your car, you are a hazardous waste hauler.

They should be put into a full cycle where industry maintains ownership of the materials. The objects must be redesigned for disassembly. When you finish with your television set, you take it back where you bought it and give it back to Sony; they recycle it into their own systems, and they stop mining mercury in South Africa. We're seeing a design for disassembly in Germany already, because it creates customer loyalty. You return the Sony, you pick up a new one. They will smell the coffee on that.

There is a third kind of product, which is the nonsellable product. Why would anyone produce a product that no one would buy?

Welcome to the wonderful world of nuclear waste. Welcome to the wonderful world of chromium tanning and leather. We should not be burying our shoes. We should be warehousing chromium's tainted leather until we know what to do with chromium. We are making products that no one should buy.

We have the three kinds of products. How does this affect our thinking about design? As an architect, I'm going to focus on the making of buildings.

Five thousand years ago, we had clay, caves, and tents. The ancients were very, very wise and practiced organizing mass, such as an adobe mud hut to work with the sunshine. They knew how thick a wall needed to be to transfer the heat of the day into the night for the evening in the winter, and how thick it needed to be to transfer the coolness of the evening into the interior in the summer. They worked with what we call thermal capacity in the walls in terms of storage and thermal lags. They worked straw in the roof to protect the heat loss in the winter and to shield the heat gain in the summer from the high sun. They made very sensible buildings within the climate in which they were located.

The Beduoin tent does five things at once. In the desert, it's 120 degrees. There is no shade, there is no air moving. The black tent is pitched so that it creates deep shade that brings your sensible temperature to 95 degrees. Also, it is a very coarse weave, which means it is a beautifully illuminated material, having a million light fixtures. Then you notice, because of the coarse weave and the black surface, the sun is creating convector currents on the outside of the black surface. The air is rising and the air gets sucked through the membranes. So now you have a breeze coming in from all sides that drops the sensible temperature down to 90 degrees. You're looking out at the white British canvas tent thinking about mad dogs. You start to wonder about what happens when it rains with those giant holes up there and you find out that the hairs swell up and it gets tight as a drum. And you can roll it up and take it with you. This is an astonishingly elegant house.

Modern architecture arrives on the scene with the advent of the large sheet of glass. It was very unfortunate that, concurrently, cheap energy became available. Architects forgot where the Sun is. I have spoken to thousands of architects. When I ask the question, "Where is true south?" I never get a hand.

In this country, we adopted a design principle that said if brute force doesn't work, you're not using enough of it. We've dealt with the glass ironically: we make glass buildings that are more about buildings than they are about people. The hope that glass would connect you to the outdoors is completely stultified by making the building sealed. We create astonishing stress in people, because they're meant to be connected to the outdoors, but they've been trapped. Indoor air quality issues are now becoming very serious. People are realizing how horrifying it can be to trap people indoors, especially with the chemicals that are being used to make things today.

We can go back to a popular statement from the early part of this century that the house is a machine for living in. If the house is a machine for living in, then an office is a machine for working in, and a church is a machine for praying in. It is a terrifying prospect. Designers are now designing for the machine and not for people. People talk about solar-heating a building. People talk about solar-heating a cathedral. You don't solar heat a cathedral. The cathedral isn't asking you for heat. The *people* are asking you for heat. Heat your feet!

We need to work with John Todd's idea that we need to work with living machines, not machines we're living in, living machines that focus on people's real needs. We need clean water. We need safe materials. We need durability. We need to work from current solar income. Let me describe a few of our projects as an example of how these issues are implicit in design decisions. In 1986, when we were hired by the Environmental Defense Fund, the executive director said at the end of the contract negotiations, "By the way, if anybody gets sick from indoor air quality, we're going to sue you."

We decided to go ahead, even though we were wondering if we should take the job. We decided it was our job to find the materials to specify to make sure it was done right. What we found is that those materials aren't there. Our manufacturers had to be trained. We experimented with paints from Germany, we worked with different kinds of lighting, we did the best we could, but we realized the entire system is essentially toxic. We're working on that.

For Paul Stuart, a men's store on Madison Avenue, we planted one thousand oak trees to replace the two English oaks that we used in the store. There's a famous story by Gregory Bateson. At New College Oxford, they had a dining hall that dated from 1639. The English oak beams, forty feet long and two feet in section, were suffering from dry rot after 350 years and they had a committee looking for trees. The veneer alone of an English oak tree is worth seven dollars a square foot. A log could be easily five hundred thousand dollars. They needed five hundred of them. They didn't have forty-foot-tall straight English oaks in England anymore. A young faculty member joined the committee and he said, "Why don't we ask the college foresters about some of the lands that have been given to Oxford?" The college foresters responded, "We've been waiting for you to ask us this question. When this building was built, the architect specified that a grove of trees be planted and maintained to replace the beams in a ceiling that would suffer from dry rot in 350 years." That is how to run a culture. My question is, did they replant them?

For Warsaw, when we designed a proposal there in a competition, the client came in, saw the model, and said "You win." We said, "We're not quite finished yet, we have to tell you about the building." The base is made from concrete that has recycled rubble from the war. It looks like limestone and it's there for visceral reasons. He said, "Fine, that's okay." The skin is recycled aluminum. We've talked to aluminum companies. We can make sure it's recycled. He said, "That's okay, that's fine." The floor heights are thirteen feet clear so we can convert the building into housing in the future. He said, "That's okay." We have opening windows. No one is more than twenty-five feet from fresh air. "That's okay." The spire is enmeshed in the clouds moving through it. And "That's okay." The geometry of the building is a clock and let's people know what the sun is doing during the year. "That's okay."

By the way, we added, you have to plant ten square miles of forest to offset the building's effects on climate change, the calculated energy cost to build it, and the energy cost to run it. So he said, "You're right, you don't win, I'll get back to you," and left. He called ten days later and said, "You win. I checked out what it would cost to plant ten square miles of trees in Poland and it turns out it is one-tenth of my advertising budget."

Walmart Corporation called us a year ago and said, "Will you help us with a store in Lawrence, Kansas?" We said, "We don't know if we can work with you. Our mandate needs to come from the top. We have to know you believe this. We also want you to be in a position to discuss the impact of Walmarts on small towns." Click.

Three days later they called back and said, "We have a question for you that's coming from the top. Are you willing to discuss the fact that people with lives have the right to buy the finest quality products even under your own terms at the lowest possible price?" We said yes. They said, "Then we can talk about the impact on small towns."

We worked with them on a store in Lawrence, Kansas. We converted the building from steel construction (which is three hundred thousand BTU's per square foot just to build) to wood construction, which uses about forty thousand, thereby saving thousands of barrels of oil just in the fabrication of the building. We decided to use only wood that came from sources that were protecting biodiversity. In our arrangements with the largest technically engineered wood product company in America, we found that the forests that once belonged to James Madison and Zachary Taylor in Virginia had been put into sustainable forestry when they died. The wood from the beams came from their forests. We set up a sustainable forestry program protecting biodiversity in Oregon to do the rest of the wood for that store.

We began to look at the toxicities of materials. After three days of meeting with engineers on the CFC issue, I gave up and said, "Everybody leave early today. Your assignment is to spend one hour with someone under the age of twelve and talk about CFC's." You will discover that what you say to CFC's is what you say to drugs, "Just say NO!" That's what the children will understand.

The next morning they came in; within an hour we figured out how to do it. We called up the air conditioning companies and said this is what we want: "We want you to go from closed to open cycles." They said, "Oh, Dupont will figure it out." We said, "You don't seem to understand. We're talking about a billion dollar order. "Oh, we can do it. We can do it right away."

For the city of Frankfort, we won a competition for a day care center that's operated by children. It's got a greenhouse roof that has five

functions like a Beduoin tent. It heats and cools itself. The children oper-
ate it. The biggest problem we've been having is with the engineers.

They say "What happens when the children forget to close the shades
and they get too hot?"

We say, "Well, they're going to open a window".

"What if they don't open a window?"

"Then they're going to close the shades."

"How do you know they're going to close the shades?"

"Because the children aren't brain-dead."

"Why can't we automate it?"

"Because it's important for the children to look at the day in the morning to see what the sun is going to do that day and then interact with it."

We enlisted the teachers in Frankfurt to get this one across. They said,
"The most important thing for us is finding things for kids to do. You give
me ten minutes of things for them to do in the morning and ten minutes
of things for them to do when they put the building to bed at night. We'll
love you for it." We also suggested to the city of Frankfort that they add
a public laundry to the project. The building does not need fossil fuels to
maintain human comfort. We can do that with glazing. We can do a building that does not need fossil fuels. We asked them to put a public laundry
in so that the parents would have a place to wait for their kids. Fifty years
from now, when there are no fossil fuels, the building will contribute hot
water to the community, thereby paying back its embodied energy mort-
gage and providing a social center.

What are the ethical implications of all this? In the history of rights,
we can trace back to the Magna Charta in 1215, when white English
noble males were given inalienable rights. With the Declaration of
Independence in 1776, rights were extended to white landowning
American males. Then we slowly move up through emancipation, universal suffrage, the Civil Rights Act, and, at last, the Endangered Species
Act of 1973. That was the first time that human beings registered the right
of something in nature to exist. It is a Declaration of Interdependence,
such as Secretary of Agriculture Henry Wallace called for in 1939.

Today the whole question of sovereignty is in flux. Everywhere sovereigns are losing control. Money is no longer in his charge. There are two
hundred thousand computers in the world controlling the value of

money. Not one sovereign can name the value of their currency. That's where the rubber meets the road and where people comunicate viscerally. I'll give you this, you give me that.

We see too that the sovereign is losing the ability to get away with telling lies. We saw that with Chernobyl. The Russians told the Swedes, if your geiger counters start to click, no big deal. But a satellite with ten-meter resolution picks up the whole event. There's Chernobyl. It's on the front page of every newspaper in the world.

What we saw at the Earth Summit in Rio is that the sovereigns have lost the ability to lead. When Maurice Strong was asked how many world leaders were at the Earth Summit, he said, "Unfortunately, we had 104 heads of states but no leaders."

Gaia Now:
Theory and Practice

PAUL MANKIEWICZ

I rreversible change can be described as evolution. And that evolution includes us. We have evolved from some lineage. We are also part of a context, a circumstance, a community that supports us. We have to rediscover our potential as beings just as we understand again our limits.

Our capacities as human beings are magnificent, as no one has described better than Tom Berry; "We have been able to act like a geological epoch performing force. We have changed the surface of the Earth whether in our image and likeness or in essentially an analog of planetesimal striking the planet."

I want to play in three parts today. I will talk about the theoretical reach of the Gaia hypothesis, about our practical work, and also about the fairly perfect split between arts, sciences, and religion in modernity.

We have been extremely good at that partisan division between realms of thought and that's of course important for getting disciplinary clarity on some issues as Descartes was very clear on himself. Clear and distinct ideas were the basis of sciences. But that clarity is probably also illusory because we can't rationalize rivers, oceans, or the planet Earth in the same way we do our own individual bodies. Those escape because they are on a scale of complexity in size and organization that is beyond what rationality can grasp.

Gaia is the extremely simple notion that the planet regulates itself by the agency of light and beings on the Earth's surface. At St. Francis' day at the Cathedral of St. John the Divine, Julie and I carry a bowl of green algae. Those beings are the oldest that we know on this Earth. So that they are a beautifully blue-green algae, we double or triple the concentration of carbon dioxide in the growth medium like the ancient Earth they grew in before oxygen was rampant. Creatures that are three and a half billion years old. They are key transformers, because they produce the oxidative capacity to run the respiration of higher currents. These creatures had inherent in their behavior, it seems, the capacity to change the Earth.

There are arguments on all sides about this, but science is based on arguments. If you think that the Earth simply runs itself because it is in the right place, the right distance from the sun (in Job, it is called the Golden Ox hypothesis), you may say the Earth happened to be the right temperature for organisms. That's very nice, but it's not a hypothesis. On the other hand, if you say organisms run the planet and are the agency of transformation, that's a hypothesis.

Think of plants: what they do, how they capture sunlight, and invest that sunlight in organic form in the soil, literally dissolving the rock in the process, with microbes that they feed below the soil. We all live within our compost heaps, literally use the stuff that holds minerals for the rest of being to utilize as part of their living fluid, their blood, their cytoplasm.

It is very simple physical chemistry. A towel is made of the plant product, cellulose. The tightness of the weave basically informs the structure's capacity to move water. A very loose weave will move water just a very short height; gathered very tightly, it would move it much higher. The weave of plant cells themselves is actually high enough and tight enough to move water to hundreds of feet. But it would move through those small openings much too slowly.

But if you take the cellulose and you drop it down into the soil it goes something like this: it pulls water in, and as it does so, it also pulls minerals into that film. When the water and minerals are in that film, it creates a living substrate of bacteria basically living on carbon molecules, hydrogen, and the waste products of plants. So the design is very simple; when you die as a plant, your being is incorporated into the transformation of the mineral of the planet into availability for other beings. People knew this from chemistry, but it was James Lovelock, and actually Tyler Volk, who looked at the way the Earth worked in terms of the way roots, minerals, plants, and oceans are interconnected.

You can throw away a leaf, and it becomes a food for beings that will dissolve the rocks to feed more beings. Or another way to say it: that leaf itself pulls water, and water is life.

What are the philosophical consequences? Hard-headed notions like complexity depend upon the number and kinds of beings in a bioregion in an ecological system, but what is that complexity like? Is complexity the competitive war of all against all? No. It turns out that what organizes the process is a cooperative exchange, because different kinds of beings can do things together that they couldn't do separately. The bacteria can dissolve the minerals of the rock surfaces; the plants can capture the sunlight but cannot dissolve the minerals of the rock surfaces; and the bacteria cannot catch the sunlight. All together, however, they become a transformer. Exchange basically leads to differences between beings and to a kind of reciprocity which has the capacity for transformation.

What practice is suggested by these ideas? A dead world, if you assume there is not much you can do. It doesn't lead to profundity or wonder in the same way that an animated world does. It is stunning to realize that native peoples everywhere who have lived in their bioregion for a period of time usually know about all of the animals and plants in their neighborhoods. It's not easy. In the southern Bronx there are 200 species of plants, in the northern Bronx and Westchester there are up to 780 species of plants. It is daunting what people have discovered in their regions, and simply lived with as their medicine, their food, as the living energy that connects them on a daily basis to their world. We have worked out a different style through technology which has lacked the capacity to meet the world with compassion and empathy, because if the world is dead, why would you?

The power of a notion like the Gaia hypothesis is that the Earth may be closer to something alive. You say, "Well it's not; it can't reproduce itself." That's true. But then how about the Hudson River? That can't reproduce itself. Is that alive? Well, yes. Is the Hudson River a unique entity, that is to say, can it appear again in time? The answer would have to be no. It's a unique entity like all complex life forms. Anything with cells with nuclei basically is a one-shot entity, and once there is sex everything is finished. Individuality becomes radical. We are different from our parents, our grandparents. Our children are different from us. We can have twins but each of those, once they have gathered a certain amount of experience, are individuated.

Literally coming into contact with some set of hydrocarbons, eating certain kinds of foods, cell surfaces change so that they simply will be different throughout their own history.

We like to see things as being in some kind of equilibrium. There is actually a great deal of individuation. The sorry truth is that we are no more unique, in a biogeochemical sense, than the algae. You say that we can think and that's power. We cannot though, take a whole class of very complex alcohols, surround them with green pigment, and take sunlight and feed the rest of the biosphere. That is an unbelievably complicated quantum process. It's what the oak tree does. It doesn't know that it is doing it. There are complicated processes which are in one sense radically different from us and in another sense they are mirror images of what we are.

The oak tree breathes out oxygen, we breathe out carbon dioxide. We breathe in oxygen, the oak tree breathes in carbon dioxide. But it doesn't actually breathe. Instead, it has feather structures called stomata along the leaf. There are as many as fifteen thousand of them per square centimeter organized in pairs, opening up into the body of the leaf. They can close or open because carbon dioxide has to dissolve in a kind of a moist surface, much as the capillaries do in our lungs.

Instead of having to breathe, which consumes lots of energy, the oak tree uses aerodynamics. The air shears off over the edges of the leaves on the outside, creating negative forces compared to the slower moving air around the middle of the leaf, simply because air runs fastest over edges. Because there is more negative pressure on the outside of the leaf, just a slight air movement will force air out of those tiny openings into the openings in the middle of the oak leaf. So we have two things: an autonomic process like breathing is a beautiful, rhythmic orienting of much of our consciousness, but the breath of a plant cell is actually directly coupled to the movement of the atmosphere. It requires no energy on the plant's part. It is simply structural. It moves atmosphere into the leaf and out of the leaf without anything but form to organize it.

That takes us to another level of what beings do, though it is hard to say how the whole Earth works. For a long time, the beings of this region extending up the Hudson as far as Albany and the Hudson Dike actually lived on the energy that flowed through this area. Organisms as far south as the tropics also lived on the energy of this region. When the migratory groups like redstarts come through in the fall, they actually live on the insects and seeds that have been produced in abundance here. The power of the energy captured here becomes incorporated into the way tropic rain forests work, because the birds down there were also gathering insects and seeds and changing the movement of material from the trees to insects to themselves and to other beings.

It doesn't seem like much, but in the dry season in the tropics when there are fewer predators and insects around, a number of caterpillars can go and eat the apex of a small tree. They eat the apex and it doesn't kill the tree, but if the tree isn't a certain size by the dry season, it dies. In other words, if there is not an insect predator to eat enough of the insects, then the tree survival rates will have to go down.

Some of those predators are fed by the creatures that move from the north through our system. The Earth is a kind of unity as well, but it depends on the integral unity of the place where we are. What could we do about that?

Let me talk a little bit about what we do at the Gaia Institute and what this region once was and maybe what it could be again. In simple terms we are a waste-to-resources enterprise. We look at different kinds of waste materials, and try to make them into something useful. That has been done in a number of ways. One example came about when the Department of Sanitation said to us, "Could you build a food waste composting system for a capital cost of under one thousand dollars per ton?" Basically we are looking at some kind of composter that takes food wastes and makes it into compost that doesn't cost a great deal. We found subsequently that no one has ever done anything like this. The cheapest off-the-shelf system is about forty thousand dollars per ton.

But not knowing that, being somewhat naive, we built one for about five hundred dollars per ton. It is essentially a garbage bag that has a space on the bottom that air comes into it. So if you just take food waste and make it into a fairly small size (it has to be shredded up a bit) and mix it with finished compost and then pile it up very gently, the material will break down to half of its weight and volume between two to four days and can no longer rot and smell disgusting. After about seven or eight days more, it can be sold as a fertilizer.

So what makes garbage disgusting essentially can be changed. We don't do it, though. People often say "Why isn't everybody doing this if this is so easy?" And of course it's not so easy. I simply started a new bacteria, and I knew how fast it could grow, and I just figured out from that how large the body was of the bacterial colony covered in about half a day, and it turns out to be, roughly speaking, something like that. I took a bunch of soil and looked at it, so we simply did that. We took stuff and got some ground-up stuff that was actually about that size, mixed it with finished compost, put a fan and inserted about the amount of air that we thought the bacteria required. In twelve hours the bag was 130 degrees and we had to double the air content because otherwise it got to be unbelievably hot. This time it went up to 180 degrees and almost self-destructed. We couldn't touch the thing. Simply because the creatures of the world will organize themselves around the movement of material.

We can stand in the way of that process, we can put chainsaws to cut down, we can put concrete and macadam in the way of life processes, but we can also actually step back and do things otherwise. This coast was probably the richest temperate estuary on the planet before we got here. Now, New Yorkers will pay fifty million dollars to put a plastic and clay cap on top of the Pelham Bay Landfill, because that's what the state-of-the-art technology says that we should do to clean it up. But all that does is keep the rain from going through the landfill. For a small percentage of that kind of money, you could actually surround the landfill with wetlands, salt marshes. We are right now designing a system for the city like that.

Why would you want to do that? Added to the landfill are thousands of pounds of ammonia. Ammonia is a toxin to the creatures on the food chain: the algae, the ciliates. It so happens that already the Hudson is actually breaking down about twenty thousand tons of ammonia each year. But by taking the area south of the landfill here and putting in about thirteen acres of wetlands, we would be recreate what the Bronx was one hundred years ago. The creatures of the salt marsh would be able to break down eight thousand times the ammonia that would ever come out of the landfill. The cost of that would be the breaking down of ammonia to nitrates and nitrogen gas and also to plant food.

It would be feeding bacteria, and then feeding creatures in the food chain that feed the oysters, the mussels, the clams, and about 70 per cent of the organisms of the whole North Atlantic. Some part of their life cycle depends upon food chains of the salt marshes. So the cost of doing this would be basically the improvement of our fisheries. The process also sequesters heavy metals and breaks down hydrocarbons and PCB's. As to the dollars and cents cost, you could spend 10 per cent of the fifth million dollar budget for capping that zone.

It's using the geometry of Euclid, the thoughts of Newton, some of our analytic capacities, but the context is different. Instead of actually trying to create something where human beings have to do something, you simply create circumstances like this world once had. And the beings organize themselves.

Other kinds of technologies can move us in some similar directions. We got into the business of composting because it seemed that New York has a tremendous resource. All of us here are involved in exchange processes called markets. Now those have been fairly destructive forces run by multinational corporations. But all beings exchange. Every being on the planet exchanges something with their circumstances. How could we take the exchange of money and food sustenance for each of us and actually make that benefit all New Yorkers?

Much as salt marshes are a transformer that could soften the edge of our coast line and turn the pollutants into food for beings again, our rooftops could become agricultural sources. We could grow plants for restoring ecological systems on roofs. We invented a composting system so that we would never have to import nutrients for fertilizer for growing food in New York because food waste has potassium, phosphate, and nitrogen in exactly the amounts plants require, because it is made from plants.

The simple idea is that by importing the food wastes from the rest of the boroughs, plus all its own food waste and the food waste of restaurants, the Cathedral could become a net exporter of food to the regions around here and also grow seedlings for the farms upstate and in New Jersey, so that they would be able to start their plants out earlier in the spring.

What about our way of dealing with storm water? Macadam does not support the holding of water, and without water you don't have beings. We suggest millions of dollars for storm sewers whose sole purpose is to move water as rapidly as possible from the city into the Hudson, East River, Long Island Sound, Jamaica Bay. Rapid movement of water is their purpose.

What could be done differently? It turns out that a place like New York (which gets more than forty inches of water per year) could readily cool itself between five to fifteen degrees throughout the summer if more water were held on and around buildings. Parks, of course, also run out of water because we run it off the land into the storm sewers. Parks, too, would be substantially cooler.

Case in point: There is a little park over in Queens. And there is a ravine that was cut by the glacier, full of exquisite, beautiful ferns and horsetails, and some lycopodium and skunk cabbage. Just a beautiful place. Then they put a roadway up on top, a school on one side, three big houses on the other, and dumped a bunch of old cars. Now it's just a weedy gulch.

The city of New York has a flooding problem. We can have a three inch rainfall in an hour and apparently every corner is under water. What to do? You could spend between ten to fifty million dollars to dig storm sewers in different places, or feed coal into the aquifier so that the storm water percolates down, or dig up the Long Island Expressway so it can go as rapidly as possible to the surrounding body of water.

Or if you simply lined the top of this ravine with clay, it could actually hold one-half to one million gallons of water that could then be let out into one wetland of cattails and rushes and another wetland that is made of ferns, wild rice, and all the mosses that used to grow there fifteen hundred years ago. The cost of that would be roughly five hundred thousand dollars. If you wanted to make an exquisitely beautiful park and do extensive landscaping, it might rise to nine hundred thousand dollars. In the end, you'd have a restored wetland no different from what was there a thousand years ago. You would also have clear drinking water, because bacteria digest viruses and break down enteric bacteria from the effluents.

The point of all this is very simple: Life depends on an engagement with circumstances. That's what supports us and has always supported us. From the eighth century to the present we have lost more and more of our history: the history of the Neolithic which coupled us with a number of plants, and the history of the Paleolithic which coupled us with all of the beings that supported us. The variety of organisms that lived back then was magnificent. That magnificence is not gone; nature still has her wildness. That wildness can't be conserved without our participation, and it can't simply be passively let go.

Our very bodies are already communicating. Each of us would die in a relatively short period of time if somebody invented a compound that killed all of the vitamin K-producing organisms in your gut. We literally could not clot our blood without vitamin K. We couldn't run about a tenth of the biochemical reactions in the body without riboflavin, half of which comes from the creatures in our gut. That's simply what's in the body. If you turn and look to your surroundings, it is much more dynamic, much more powerful: there are about one thousand species of plants, just within your purview. In every gram of soil there are ten million bacteria. Those are doing something and actually would do something even in our immediate circumstances, but they will not do it if we eliminate the conditions of life. That has been the fundamental error in rationality.

God's Oiconomia

THE REV. MINKA SHURA SPRAGUE

In the name of God, master architect, ultimate choreographer, lover of all saints, all souls. Amen.

Here it all is. We have talked Sunday after Sunday about the world after the Earth Summit in Rio. How it is. How to be in Creation. How to be with Creation, aware. With the nations, tribes, and peoples gathered, living on this planet we call home, Earth. After Rio, a new awareness of the fragile, the interdependence of what we call life, in what we call our world. And then it is the Feast of All Saints this Sunday for the talking of the world after Rio. Remembrance and honor for all who have gone before us. A festival day. All Hallows, All Saints' holding in memory all saints—God holds all souls in design. And it's baptism, the consecration of a new Christian life beginning this day on All Saints', All Souls', in a world after Rio, signed and sealed as Christ's and forever. A new Christian life beginning this day for some of us remembered this day for All Saints, All Souls. Renewed this day for those of us who have baptism deep, deep in the marrow of our bones. This is ordination for us all, the baptized. Ordination into Christ's eternal priesthood. Committed and pledged and vowed and sent forth in Christian stewardship, All Saints, All Souls. And the Russians are not coming, they are here. They're here for baptism in the festival of All Saints and the world after Rio. And so is Madeline, along with the Russians, and the baptism and the celebration of All Saints, All Souls, in this world after Rio. Author, theologian, teacher, sister, colleague, and friend here with us, handed stewardship commitment someday. A time to commit energy and the currency of time and money, greenbacks if you will, a time to commit to the life of the church in time and money for the coming year.

And an election that matters is around the corner, this baptism, this All Saints' Sunday. In the world after Rio, we have a vote that matters. And they are running. Running as we gather here over the bridges and through the boroughs—pretty good for the *New York Times*, right? "Over the bridges and through the boroughs." Running, running somewhere between the (Verrazano's) Narrow and West 67th Street. Here it all is. Divinely designed, masterfully architected, choreographed, danced by the power of God's own breath. Running, running on the energy, the currency of God's love. Fit, coherent, coinherent, says the Dean, divinely designed, interdependent, interconnected, interwoven, one body. One body. All of it. All things in Heaven and all things on Earth. Please pledge All Saints, All Souls, all the women in this actor's life in Madeline's new books, all the Russians, signed and sealed as Christ's forever, every tree in the southern hemisphere, every syllable, every tongue, everyone running between the (Verrazano) Narrows and Central Park, suppertime in Jerusalem this very moment, and who knows out there beyond the Milky Way? One body. It all—here it all is—it fits.

Now this was true before Rio, too. This one body, divinely designed. This one body danced in God's breath on the energy of love. It was in place, actually, a long time before the starting signal on the Verazzano Bridge. It was in place before there was a Russia, or Ross Perot, or pledge cards, or women gathered for a story. It was there very long before the unions out of which the baptized are born and the All Saints have gone before us, long before. Long before waters separated from waters and a greater light given dominion over us all. What is new is this: in the world after Rio, All Saints, All Souls, we are more aware of being aware. Aware of one body, Earth's body, and our own. Aware that it all is divinely designed. Aware of coherent, coinherent, interdependent, interwoven. Now the New Testament has a word, one word for all of this. The pledge of money and time, God's design, the way we walk our ordinations are the baptized. One word in the New Testament for it all: *Oiconomia*. Economy, the New Testament calls it. This is God's plan, *oiconomia*. *Oiconomia* is what the apostle says he is to do in Corinth, care for the community. *Oiconomia* is the way a householder manages the accounts. *Oiconomia* is the way the servant manages the tasks. The *oiconomia* is stewardship: the pledge of money and time. It's the way, the shape, the design, the dance, the pledge card. All one word, the very large and the very small. Our call to stewardship, to *oiconomia*. Life after Rio is to know this, to know that every breath we take and every step we make is *oiconomia*. One body, one design. *Oiconomia* life is spending our energy, which is God's own love and God's own breath, aware of aware. *Oiconomia* life, Christian stewardship, and dance in the divine design is committing our green and our backs. The currencies of our energy. Committing our green and our backs, and our awareness, our energy, which runs on God's love. Committing them to this life, this divine design, knowing that every exhalation and every dollar matters, that every can recycled counts, that every word spoken or written signifies, that every vote elects, that every smile heals. Every breath we take, every step we make. *Oiconomia,* life, stewardship and dance in the divine design is knowing that it fits and belongs more than we can see, sometimes more than we can imagine. And we walk it by faith.

Here it all is. The world after Rio, All Saints, All Souls. Signed and sealed forever as Christ's own. Ordained to an eternal priesthood. Ordained to *oiconomia,* one body life. Where All Saints after Rio, and Russians and runners and certain women and certain men, indeed maybe all women and all men, somewhere between the moon and the Milky Way, belong, by faith in one body in love. By divine design. So, isn't it all, every breath we take, every step we make, pretty good news?

November 1, 1992

On Food-Sharing,
Communion, and
Human Culture

WILLIAM IRWIN THOMPSON

On my way to the Cathedral this time, I decided not to fly quickly to New York, but to drive across the country, to take the time to see those places across America where a new spirit is coming into place, where a new relationship between nature and culture is coming into being with its own vision of a new Heaven and a new Earth. So I drove from the Lindisfarne Institute in Colorado to the Land Institute in Salina, Kansas, to the Meadowcreek Project in Fox, Arkansas, to Wendell Berry's farm in Port Royal, Kentucky, and then on to the meeting of the E. F. Schumacher Society in western Massachusetts, and finally to the New Alchemy Institute on Cape Cod. And in all of these places the conversation was of the coming crisis of American agriculture, of the loss of the soil and the mining of water, the draining of the Ogalala aquifer, the greenhouse effect and its consequent changing of the climate. And throughout all of these conversations there was a sense that the seventies, with its short-lived fads of cultural change and consciousness-raising, were over. In the eighties people are concerned only with industrial economics, with inflation, interest rates, and unemloyment. Now to speak of ecology is to speak, not of the wind, but to the wind.

Looking back, the conversation with the poet Wendell Berry seems to stand out as a voice in the wilderness. If anyone is a prophet these days, a voice speaking for the Earth against the machines, it is Wendell Berry. In his book, *The Unsettling of America*, he has brought together poetry and social analysis in a single vision. With a note of fatigue still abiding in enduring strength, Wendell said that as time goes on the Christian doctrine of "the Remnant" begins to take on a new descriptive power for our age. The best that the individual can do in these times is to bear witness to the truth, and to try to do the best one can with the piece of the Earth for which one is responsible.

Here there is no exhaustion of the soul in media manipulation or mass movements of consciousness-raising. His words impressed themselves upon me, for his mood matched my own, and his assessment of what we all had done and not done in the seventies, also matched my own. In the seventies many people thought that if one simply got the message out, that was enough. We are all children of a media society; we think that if someone is on national television that is a real piece of work, the equivalent of a true achievement in human creativity. We believe too much in this idolatry of the media. We think that human culture is constituted in this conference, that press release, and this media event. Human achievement is measured in the amount of television coverage one can get. And through it all is the assumption that if one can simply get enough, then the world will be changed, and one's personal fantasy will become the collective reality.

So whether it was the case of the Club of Rome on the side of the powerful, or the Findhorn Foundation on the side of the powerless, the activities of the seventies were exercises in the manipulation of images. The ancient Chinese sages have said that: "Reversal is the movement of Tao." And so the eighties do seem to be the reversal of the seventies. Some of us have become stuck in the seventies, have become conference junkies jet-setting from one consciousness-raising event to another. But the zeitgeist has changed, and New Age sentiments seem out of key. The cotton candy optimism that things will all come out pink and fluffy won't do.

Under the pressure of economic and political crises, there is a stiffening and a hardening of position, as all postures become defensive ones. Certainly in the part of the world in which I live there are survivalist communities who speak with growing anticipation and excitement of The Latter Days. There people are storing weapons and food and are prepared to kill so that they may live. They do not look at the Christian doctrine of the Remnant with compassion: they simply elect themselves to the company of the divinely chosen ones. In Wendell Berry's case, the idea of the Remnant is a call to serve the Earth, to be one of the last, if need be, who will continue to bear witness to the truth of human love in an age of hate. The survivalist, by contrast, feels that he can elect himself into the Remnant, and with enough food and weapons he can force his way into eternal life. He thinks that he is escaping the follies of the modern world, but, in fact, he is in miniature a caricature of the modern nation-state. For what today is a nation-state but a survivalist community? The technocratic managers speak of triage and calculate who shall survive and who shall not. The scientist Garret Hardin says, in effect, that we deceive ourselves in acts of compassion, for we think that when we send food to people in other parts of the world that we are helping. But, he claims, we are only increasing the number of the suffering; better to drop atom bombs on the starving millions of Southeast Asia, for then, the scientist of triage points out, their suffering would only be momentary and not generational.

The survivalist communities in Colorado or Montana are simply vulgar and lower-class versions of the ideas expressed in the mathematics of the policy analysts of think-tanks and governments. But in both communities we come across the notion that the ego can elect itself into the Remnant, and through the grace of religion or science, it shall survive.

In reality, these two images of the human community, one of compassion and food-sharing, and the other of storing weapons and food, have been with us for a very long time. In social science these two different images determine how one thinks about the dawn of humanity and the very beginning of human culture. One group of anthropologists says that it was the weapon that made us human. As we took stone tools in hand, we fell from animal innocence and turned to confront nature armed with the first technology. We hurled ourselves up into a new technological level, and everything that was left behind was the primitive. And so, in this view, human culture is created and determined by technology, and the most basic technology of all is the weapon.

Of course, any story about human beginnings is a myth, even if it is a scientific myth, and as such it tells us more about the culture making the description than the culture being described. The social scientists who make these sorts of descriptions about human origins also see the present as a condition in which a new technology is hurtling a new group of humans into a higher level, and everything that is left behind is the primitive. The technologist can turn upon traditional humanity to say: "We are the highest, the most advanced; you are simply the sloughed-off remains of an old animal nature." For these people, the arms race is neither a necessary evil nor a peculiar pathology; it is the driving force of human evolution itself. So do not look to them to sit down at a negotiating table to seek ways to throw their weapons away.

Fortunately, there is another scientific vision of human origins, one associated with the work of the anthropologist, Glynn Isaacs. The theory has it that the protohominids carried their food to a safe shelter and there, in an act of community definition, they shared their food. From this perspective, the primary act of human culture is food-sharing. And here we can see that the communion we are about to partake in today is an ancient memory. In the sharing of food we most truly perform our basic humanity. Thus the Jewish *seder* or the Christian eucharist expresses a transformation of nature into culture, not with a weapon, but with a gift. When the grape is transformed into wine, or when the grain is transformed into bread, nature is transformed into culture. When Christ calls us to take communion in memory of him, he is reminding us that in the sharing of food we can realize that we are all involved in a common life. There can be no "us and them."

So the image of the Mystical Body of Christ is basically an ecological vision of a shared life. And so it is in other religions as well. In the ancient Mexican myths of Quetzalcoatl, the gods take food, chew it, and then place it on our lips, as mothers do with infants. This is a beautiful mythic expression of the relationship of the Sun and the Earth, for the gods of air must first chew the solar energy before they pass it down to us. If we tried to eat the food of the Sun directly, we would grow incorrectly, we would get cancer. And so the solar energy must be chewed and transformed by Gaia, and as the energy is transformed into living plants, it is turned into food for innumerable beings. Thus food is not an object to be stored and hoarded, it is a process, a relationship. As it says in the Upanishads:

> Earth is food. Air lives on earth.
> Earth is air. Air is earth. They
> are food to one another.

The science of ecology is a science, not of material objects, but living relationships. It is also a science of the rediscovery of mythic insights. *Eco* means "home"; *logos* means "word"; *ecology* is the homeword, the homeward science. We go back to our ancient home to rediscover in the language of science what we once knew in the language of myth. Ecology is thus the science of reconciliation, a science of the healing of culture with nature, of the word with the home, of thought with the body. At its height, ecology is a resacralization of science, a new vision of the relationship of the unique part with the Universal Whole. Just as physics was basic to the engineering of an industrial society, so now ecology is basic to the stewardship of a new metaindustrial society. In this new world view, the world is not made out of matter, but music. Objects are not the constitutive elements of reality, relationships are. In the process philosophy of this new world view, science is not simply a matter of separation, analysis, and control, but of expression, synthesis, and co-operation.

And so through this new science there is hope that even in the face of the depressing tyranny of industrial materialism that something else is at work in the world. We do not need to fear science to say that we are truly spiritual only when we are unscientific. We do not need to be threatened by technology, for there is another kind of science in which the tool is simply a tool, and not a system of idolatry, a *techné-logos.* Just as once long ago the tool was used in a culture of food-sharing, so now tools can be used in a culture of communion. It is so easy when only tools survive as pieces of altered rock to think only in terms of technology as the definition of culture. In fact, most archaeologists make this mistake. They forget that the tool was deeply submerged in a culture, and that the tool was no more the culture than the Greek alphabet is Plato's *Timaeus.* We need, through an act of the imagination, to put the tool back into its proper context, not simply in the most ancient past, but now in the most immediate present.

Fortunately for us, it does seem as if anthropology is moving away from reductionism, and is coming to a new understanding of the cultural context of an artifact. In a recent issue of *Nature*, Henry Bunn remarked, "The documentation of meat-eating and the concentration of bones at particular places by early hominids lends strong support to the foodsharing model proposed by Isaacs."[1]

This image of food-sharing that is elaborated as the foundation of human culture is also being elaborated as a basic force in cellular evolution. In Lynn Margulis's recent book, *Symbiosis and Cell Evolution*, she takes the process of food-sharing all the way down to the level of the cell: "Food scarcity in nature probably selects for the symbionts over the separate partners." And in speaking of the importance of symbiosis itself, she notes: "Symbiosis has affected the course of evolution as profoundly as biparental sex."[2] So even in our cells, even in the secret life of our own mitochondria, we can see a vision of communion and transformation.

Now it was this work of Lynn Margulis that influenced Lewis Thomas to see the whole planet as a single cell, and to see ourselves as humans, as simply organelles within a cell.[3] And that is the right way to look at it, because in this view there can be no "us and them." You cannot seal in one part of humanity, hoarding food and exporting industrial poisons, and think that these will not come back to poison the whole. We all breathe the air others exhale. The web of life is a tissue of relationships; there is no way to wall in the ego or the factory, to have profits safely here, but pollution securely over there.

All of us in industrial society have inherited a description of the world that is simply false. Whether as scientists or Christians, or both together, we have to see that everywhere new information is coming in to show us just how false and dangerous this old industrial world view truly is. The world of natural processes, human culture, and planetary dynamics is a world of communion. The basic sacrament that we celebrate as Christians is a celebration of the transformation of death into new life. We are all members in the Mystical Body of Christ, and so in sharing food together on a planetary scale, as we will have to do in the eighties, we acknowledge that we are all food to one another. In death we pass over into food in the Earth. Civilized man with his developed ego tries to deny death, tries to deny connections, by building walls and containers, and that ultimate container, the tomb. Christ in His death celebrated the transformation, rejected the containment of the tomb, and became the bread and wine of a sacramental life.

In the days before civilization, the individual was placed in a tumulus that was made to look like the body of the Great Mother. From the Great Mother we come, to the Great Mother we return. There were no individuals, all were equal children in the clan, and so the bones in the tumulus were all jumbled up together. Then came the rise of civilization, with its standing armies and military heroes, and suddenly the tomb of the great hero appears on the scene of history. Now there was an ego with a name that needed a container and a monument. The transformation of the unique in the universal, of the many in the One of the Great Mother was denied, and the king was sealed in his tomb with all his servants and his new bronze age military technology.

This is the tradition we have inherited. The first work of Western literature is the Gilgamesh Epic, and Gilgamesh is the great hero who rejects Ishtar, slays the spirit of the forest, and cuts himself off from the cycles of nature in the walled container of the city. Having slain the spirit of nature, he then wonders why he is so afflicted with death. Gilgamesh wanted to make a name for himself by slaying the spirit of the forest, but a name, like a tomb, is simply a container for the ego; it is the name of the thing that dies. Gilgamesh became obsessed with death, as we have ever since in all the works of Western literature that have followed his story. But now at the other end of Western civilization we are ready for a new understanding, and the science of ecology has come in to teach us that if we slay the spirit of the forest and live behind the great walls of the city, then there is no way to avoid becoming obsessed with death.[4]

As the science of reconciliation, ecology is trying to work toward the transformation of industrial society in the creation of a new world view. It is naturally clashing with the old world view, the world view of industrial culture. I think that in the middle of the eighties the clash of these two world views will become intense, as more and more evidence of industrial planetary damage begins to become undeniable, except to the blind captains of industry. The second half of this decade will, I think, be a period of black and white polarization, a period very much like the forties. Indeed, we will not have seen such a confrontation of good and evil since the days of Hitler. On the one side is the ecological science of Eugene Odum, Lewis Thomas, Lynn Marqulis, James Lovelock, Glynn Isaacs, Wes and Dana Jackson, and John and Nancy Todd. On the other side are the technological apologetics for triage, the genetic engineering of plants and populations, sociobiological management, and the centralized power (both political and nuclear) of an authoritarian technocratic state. As the early propoganda for this culture, *Omni* magazine declares: "The scientific wizardry of this new technological era will define our world for us." Now as this magazine branches out from supermarkets to a television series, it is trying to lay the groundwork for the public acceptance and worship of an authoritarian technological society.

What we are heading into, I believe, is the climax of Western civilization, and in this crescendo of noise and music, will be heard a recapitulation of all the the themes of human culture, from Isaacs's hominization of the primates to Teilhard's "planetization of mankind." And since history is often the unconscious performance of myth, we will see again another battle of the Archangel of Light, Michael, with the dark dragon of matter. It will be an archetypal battle of the light of compassion against the darkness of technological materialism, of the compassionate Remnant versus the self-elected elite sealed into their containers of grain silos, missile silos, and survivalist communities. This will be the ultimate test for humanity, to see whether we are to be dismembered by technology, or remembered in Christ.

November 1, 1981

Notes

Dr. Thompson's original sermon was an oral presentation in which he spoke freely from a few notes. This transcription is an edited version in which the informal nature of the original has been refined for the purposes of publication.

1. Glynn Isaacs, "The Food-Sharing Behavior of ProtoHuman Hominids," *Scientific American* 238/4 (April, 1978): 90-108. Henry T. Bunn, "Archaeological Evidence for Meat-Eating by Plio-Pleistocene Hominids from Koobi Fora and Olduvai Gorge," *Nature*, 291 (June 18, 1981): 576.

2. Lynn Margulis, *Symbiosis and Cell Evolution* (San Francisco: Freeman, 1981), 162, 191.

3. Lewis Thomas, *Lives of a Cell* (New York: Viking, 1974), 5.

4. This discussion is rather compressed: for a full presentation, see the author's *The Time Falling Bodies Take to Light: Mythology, Sexuality, and the Origins of Culture* (New York: St. Martin's, 1981), chap. IV, 181-208; also 264-67.

CONTRIBUTORS

Mary Catherine Bateson is Clarence Robinson Professor in Anthropology and English at George Mason University. She is an Honorary Colleague of the Cathedral and a member Lindisfarne Association. Her most recent book is *Peripheral Visions: Learning along the Way.*

The Rev. Carla Berkedal was an Episcopal priest in parish ministry full-time from 1980–91, including being Canon Pastor at St. Mark's Cathedral, Seattle. Founder and Executive Director of Earth Ministry in Seattle, she is also interim associate rector of Immanuel Parish, Mercer Island, and the mother of two sons.

The Rev. Thomas Berry is president of the American Teilhard Association for the Human Future. His seminal work, *The Dream of the Earth,* is among the most passionate statements of the case for a sacred vision of ecology.

Dr. René Dubos (1902–82), the bacteriologist who isolated the first antibiotic drug, was among the great scientists of this century. He was well-known for his reflections about man's place on earth. He was an Honorary Colleague of the Cathedral of St. John the Divine.

John Kenneth Galbraith is Paul M. Warburg Professor of Economics (Emeritus) at Harvard University. He was U. S. ambassador to India during the Kennedy Administration and has authored thirty books.

The Rev. Canon Jeffrey Golliher is coordinator of the René Dubos Consortium for Sacred Ecology at the Cathedral of St. John the Divine. He is a leader among the new generation of priests devoted to an ecological view of creation.

Al Gore, Jr., is the vice president of the United States and a key advisor to the Cathedral-based National Religious Partnership for the Environment.

William Bryant Logan is writer-in-residence and Director of Communications at the Cathedral of St. John the Divine. His *Dirt* has just been published by Riverhead Books, a division of Putnam.

James E. Lovelock is co-originator of the Gaia Hypothesis and a leading student of planetary ecology. The party to celebrate the publication of his first book, *Gaia,* was held at the Cathedral.

Amory B. Lovins is director and founder of the Rocky Mountain Institute, a leading ecological think-tank. He is a member of the Lindisfarne Association.

William McDonough is a "green" architect, whose public and private projects have won praise for their environmental responsibility.

Paul Mankiewicz is executive director of the Gaia Institute, a Cathedral-based organization that both directs a program of talks regarding the Gaia Hypothesis and works practically to restore the watershed in the New York area. He is a member of the Lindisfarne Association.

Robert Kinloch Massie, Jr., is Henry Luce Fellow in theology at the Harvard Divinity School and director of the Harvard Project on Business, Values, and the Economy.

Dean James Parks Morton is Dean of the Cathedral of St. John the Divine in New York City. Sometimes known as the "Great Dean," he has made the Cathedral an international leader in sacred ecology.

The Right Rev. Sir Paul Reeves, Jr., is the Episcopal Archbishop of New Zealand. He held the International Cathedra at the Cathedral of St, John the Divine during his tenure in New York as the Anglican Observer to the United Nations.

Carl Sagan is the David Duncan Professor of Astronomy and Space Sciences at Cornell University and is among the leading cosmologists of our time. Author of numerous books and the winner of the Pulitzer Prize, he was also host of the PBS series, *Cosmos*, based upon his book of the same name.

The Rev. Minka Shura Sprague is Professor of New Testament and Biblical Languages at the New York Theological Seminary, and a Deacon of the Cathedral of St. John the Divine.

Brother David Steindl-Rast, O. C. B., is an Honorary Canon of the Cathedral and a Lindisfarne Fellow.

Maurice Strong was the Secretary-General of the United Nations Conference on Environment and Development (UNCED), held in 1992 in Rio de Janeiro.

William Irwin·Thompson is founder and head of the Lindisfarne Association and a professor at the California Institute of Integral Studies. He is also an Honorary Colleague of the Cathedral.

Timothy C. Weiskel is director of the Harvard Seminar on Environmental Values at Harvard Divinity School and a research fellow at the Center of Science and International Affairs at Harvard's John F. Kennedy School of Government.